10-28-82

BUSINESS EDUCATION
AND ACCOUNTANCY

This is a volume in the Arno Press collection

THE DEVELOPMENT OF CONTEMPORARY ACCOUNTING THOUGHT

Advisory Editor
Richard P. Brief

Editorial Board
Gary John Previts
Basil S. Yamey
Stephen A. Zeff

*See last pages of this volume
for a complete list of titles.*

BUSINESS EDUCATION
AND ACCOUNTANCY

CHARLES WALDO HASKINS

EDITED BY

FREDERICK A. CLEVELAND

ARNO PRESS
A New York Times Company
New York • 1978

Editorial Supervision: LUCILLE MAIORCA

———◆———

Reprint Edition 1978 by Arno Press Inc.

Reprinted from a copy in the University of
    Illinois Library

THE DEVELOPMENT OF CONTEMPORARY ACCOUNTING THOUGHT
ISBN for complete set: 0-405-10891-5
See last pages of this volume for titles.

Manufactured in the United States of America

———◆———

Library of Congress Cataloging in Publication Data

Haskins, Charles Waldo, 1852-1903.
  Business education and accountancy.

  (The Development of contemporary accounting thought)
  Reprint of the ed. published by Harper, New York.
  1. Business education. 2. Accounting. I. Cleve-
land, Frederick Albert, 1865-1946. II. Title.
II. Series.
HF1106.H35   1978   650   77-87272
ISBN 0-405-10900-8

CHARLES WALDO HASKINS

BUSINESS EDUCATION
AND ACCOUNTANCY

BY

CHARLES WALDO HASKINS, C.P.A., L.H.M.

LATE DEAN OF THE NEW YORK UNIVERSITY SCHOOL
OF COMMERCE, ACCOUNTS, AND FINANCE

EDITED BY

FREDERICK A. CLEVELAND, Ph.D.

WHARTON SCHOOL OF FINANCE AND COMMERCE
UNIVERSITY OF PENNSYLVANIA

NEW YORK AND LONDON
HARPER & BROTHERS PUBLISHERS
1904

CONTENTS

INTRODUCTION

IT has long been recognized that the old-time treatises on Political Economy have little in common with the experience of business men. An assignable reason for this is that these works were not, and from their very nature and inception could not pretend to be, treatises on subjects of immediate business interest. They fall more properly within the field of Politics—that department of learning which attempts to inquire into questions of public welfare. The "political" economist has not attempted to collect and to classify the data of business; his interest has been in "political" economic questions. The problems of Political Economy are protection, free-trade, currency and banking reform, conflicts of capital and labor, etc. —subjects of public or of broadly social bearing; its point of departure has been one of national or social expediency; its purpose is to win converts to a political òr social creed. The method of Political Economy, therefore, has been partisan—its literary and rhetorical form in the nature of special pleading directed towards legal and social reform.

INTRODUCTION

Failure to appreciate the true character of the voluminous literature of Political Economy has led many to conclude that all attempts made to create a scientific business literature have failed, and, further, that the facts and relations of business are not proper subjects for scientific inquiry. It is taken for granted that all economic writings are "theoretical"—"a worthless encumbrance to the library of a business man." Modern research, however, is beginning to dispel this illusion. Science has turned to the field of business for its data. It has developed treatises on commerce, transportation, banking practice, insurance, and other specific employments, and has brought the business man to recognize the possibilities and advantages of broader training. A "science" of Economics— a science whose aim it is to bring together a body of well-digested information on subjects of business —is beginning to force itself on the attention of men of affairs. The *science* of Economics has thus far been developed, in the main, by business specialists—men actively engaged in and in close touch with affairs. The actuary has accumulated much information concerning mortality and other casualties as a basis for business judgments concerning insurance; the accountant has reduced much of the data of finance to a system of records; the banker has given to his profession a digest of banking experience; other specialists have compiled data and established conclusions which serve as premises for thinking. Unfortunately, the last to recognize and to respond to the growing demand for *science* in business, and to accord a place to business education, has been the academician.

This volume has been prepared not alone as a memorial to Mr. Haskins. Better warrant is found in the fact that it represents the most advanced thought of those not actively engaged in the teaching profession on the subject of business training and on the possibility of raising high professional standards in what may be called business specialties. And if we are to draw conclusions from his published expressions, we find, clearly recognized, at least three branches of professional service in business which have no adequate educational support. The first of these is Accountancy—already recognized by the laws of five American States. The second business profession indicated is Finance —including banking, insurance, and other well-established and clearly defined financial specialties. The third is Business Administration. As pointed out by Mr. Haskins, education has not kept pace with the demands of the time. In many instances scientific inquiry is wholly wanting and professional education has no literary basis of which to avail itself.

The failure to provide groups of professional instruction has not been so much for lack of individual specialization as from refusal on the part of institutions of learning to recognize the professional scope and bearing of such training. One result of the failure to grasp the possibilities of organizing professional groups of instruction has been to leave the educational specialist in Economics to work alone in some non-professional cultural group. Another result has been to discourage specialization in economic research and to make it impossible in many instances to find trained educators for this class of professional instruction. This last result has a serious bearing on the establishment of professional groups in institutions of learning.

During the current year at least five American university presidents have attempted to bring together men who had pursued a business specialty, and who were capable of professional instruction in supplementary relation. In each case ambition was thwarted on account of the scarcity of scientific men in the field. Not that there are not enough of trained specialists in the country to make up one complementary group, for if we examine the curricula of institutions of learning to know what is actually being offered, it will be found that a great variety of specialization is being carried on. An aggregate of instruction offered, if brought into one professional group, would appear about as follows: In the special field of Accountancy—(1) the principles of accounting; (2) book-keeping, or accounting practice with special application to banking, mercantile accounts, manufacturing accounts, etc.; (3) the installation of accounts; (4) auditing; (5) the history of Accountancy. In the field of Finance— (1) money and credit; (2) domestic and foreign exchange; (3) banking practice; (4) banking law; (5) history of banking; (6) investments and speculation; (7) railroad finance; (8) financing of industrial trusts and corporations; (9) history of panics and depressions; (10) general financial history; (11) methods of public funding; (12) national revenues and expenditures; (13) State revenues and expenditures; (14) municipal revenues and expenditures. In the field of Business Administration— (1) the organization and management of industry; (2) industrial processes; (3) transportation and legislation relating to railways; (4) American commerce; (5) European commerce; (6) elementary commercial law; (7) mining, besides the collateral subjects of commercial and economic geography, industrial chemistry, mechanics, mathematics, architecture, etc. Moreover, the profession of law has established a curriculum covering every detail of business, and this, again, is divided into specialties that carry research to the highest degree of refinement with reference to the rules governing business relations and transactions for profit. Technological science has advanced with the demands of the time for a thorough knowledge of the physical facts of industry, while mathematics has developed far enough to give satisfactory conclusion to every calculative judgment.

It is not, therefore, a lack of material from which to build up a single complementary professional group of such breadth of training as to command the respect and praise of men of affairs, but the fact that the few who have undertaken specialization in the data of business have local institutional interests or other ties which makes the assembling of a complementary group next to impossible. Let us assume that there were only enough of trained specialists in Physiology, Bacteriology, Pathology, Anatomy, Surgery, etc., to man one institution, and these were scattered over a wide territory; the impossibility of undertaking professional medical instruction and of maintaining the present professional standards is apparent. Let us go to the field of Biology or Chemistry; here we find thousands of specialists at work on the data of these subjects, bringing them together into such relation that plant life and chemical reaction may be understood. The facts in the field of business are just as susceptible of classification and co-ordination. Each department and subdivision of the general subjects, Accounting, Finance, and Business Administration, above suggested, has possibilities of development into a separate, highly specialized science. Many of these subjects suggested are susceptible of still more minute subdivision for scientific research. The art of investment, for example, will never reach its highest level till special research has been applied to its narrowest interests. Real-estate investments, municipal investments, insurance investments, investments in private companies, etc., have already been differentiated in practice; and practice will profit from scientific specialized research in the same way that General Surgery has profited from Eye-and-Ear Surgery, Oral Surgery, Nasal Surgery, Abdominal Surgery, etc.

The line of progress has been suggested: Give to business a thousand recruits in scientific research, give to the teaching profession scientific business literature as a basis for instruction, give to each institution for higher instruction a professional group for preliminary training, and those who are looking towards business as a career will find in the university opportunities for culture on a plane with Letters and Art, and new business professions will take rank with Law, Medicine, Chemistry, Architecture, and Engineering—those which in the past have developed around ideals of higher service to mankind.

A posthumous collection of isolated essays and addresses, when brought together in one volume, must necessarily lack somewhat in continuity. But a life interest may be found running through them all.   The two essays on the History of Accountancy were only the beginning of what Mr. Haskins had hoped to put into literary form on the subject.   In these he did not attempt to work from original resources—simply to collect the results obtained by scientific men working in the records of History and Archæology; from these results he has drawn the data for his own subject.   With all this lack of continuity, even in their fragmentary state, these essays and addresses must take high rank among the literature of Business Education and Accountancy.

F. A. C.

PHILADELPHIA, *June* 20, 1903.

BUSINESS EDUCATION AND ACCOUNTANCY

I

BIOGRAPHICAL SKETCH

ON Friday evening, January 2, 1903, the subject of our sketch was sitting at the head of
an elaborately spread table in one of the private
dining-rooms of the Manhattan Club, New York.
Around him, as guests, were the members of the
Committee on Uniform Municipal Accounting of
the National Municipal League. The meeting was
an adjourned one, the first session of this call having
been held in Philadelphia the last week of December,
and, as the work in hand could not be brought to a
conclusion before the members were drawn away by
business engagements, Mr. Haskins's generosity and
hospitality were accepted for its completion. It
was near midnight when those present said good-
night to their host—a man of commanding physique,
by far the largest and, as he then appeared, the
most rugged one in the company. The next day
he was sick with pneumonia; and a week later the

sad news went out that Charles Waldo Haskins was dead. Messages expressing the bereavement of friends and sympathy for his immediate family and associates, tributes of affectionate regard, and the presence of those—leaders in his own profession, in business, and in institutions of learning—who followed his bier to its resting - place but faintly suggest the many who felt and silently suffered the shock caused by his death. In their memory Mr. Haskins still lives, a cherished friend, a wise counsellor, a strong, vigorous champion of right, an inspiration to higher attainment.

If we look upon life from Mr. Haskins's own viewpoint, small importance will be given to ancestry as a criterion for judgment of manly quality. Mr. Haskins was a democrat in ideals, an individualist in principle. In association, the first canon of his faith was "to estimate a man for what he proves himself to be worth." But life is little more than a group of habits, and the habits which make for greatness are largely acquired in early life. It is in this relation, therefore, using his own standards, that we find reference to ancestry justifiable. The background for a life portrait of the man is found in the natural characters and in the habits of body and of mind acquired from birth, and from early association. Both of these bear a direct relation to ancestry; natural characters, as well as habits of body and of mind, pass down from generation to generation—the first by inherited tendency, the second by training.

For the deepest shadows and for the most obscure parts of the background of our portrait we look to tradition. Our records are not clear; even tradition is in doubt as to whether his first American ancestor came to Boston from England direct or by way of the Virginia province. With his arrival at Boston, however, personal relations begin to take on some detail. From colonial record is gleaned the fact that Robert Haskins, of Boston, married Sarah, daughter of Philip Cook, of Cambridge, in 1728. We learn, also, that John Haskins, born to Robert and Sarah in 1729, came to be a man of influence in this provincial town; that at the outbreak of the struggle between England and France for territorial control he was seventeen years old, but none too young to be fired with the spirit of patriotism; that at eighteen he entered the service of a privateer, carrying letters of marque, bound for the West Indies, and in turn was prisoner to France and Spain. The same zeal for defence of principle led him, in later years, to take an active part in colonial resistance to British rule. He was a member of the "Sons of Liberty" and other local societies, which brought him in contact with the Adamses, Josiah Quincy, Edward Case, Joseph Warren, and others whose aggressive measures in the cause of liberty and home rule served to leaven the lump

3

of conservative loyalty and finally to bring Massachusetts into clash with royal arms. As a man of military training, his services were enlisted in the local militia—that body of citizen soldiers which was first to take an armed stand for independence. At Lexington he ranked as captain in the "Boston Regiment." His regular vocation was merchant, and as such he gained a reputation for integrity and fair dealing with his fellows—so far did he retain public esteem that he is referred to locally as "Honest John Haskins." This much we know of the energy and devotion to principle of the second ancestor of the American line. His wife, Hannah Upham, was a great-granddaughter of Lieutenant Phineas Upham, of Massachusetts, who died in King Philip's War; she was also descended from Rose Dunster, sister of Rev. Henry Dunster, first president of Harvard College. Through her mother she was descended from John Howland, one of the signers of the compact aboard the *Mayflower*, and active and prominent as a Massachusetts Bay Colony official. She also traced her ancestry to John Waite, who for eighteen years sat in the Massachusetts House of Deputies, of which he was made Speaker in 1684.

The third in American line, and great-grandfather of Mr. Haskins, was Robert Haskins, son of John Haskins the patriot, above mentioned. He, like his father, was a prominent and successful Boston merchant. This Robert Haskins married Rebecca, daughter of the Rev. William Emerson, who built the "Old Manse," made famous by Hawthorne, and who occupied it during the Battle of Lexington—of which he was an eye-witness, and later the annalist—and who, after years of patriotic endeavor leading up to the revolutionary struggle, laid down his life for independence while serving as chaplain at Ticonderoga, 1776. His daughter Rebecca, wife of Robert Haskins, was named after her great-grandmother, Rebecca, daughter of Cornelius Waldo, who was the aunt of Ralph Waldo Emerson, and was descended from a line of eminent jurists and scholars, several of whom were among the founders of New England.

The fourth in the American line, and grandfather of Professor Haskins, was Thomas Waldo Haskins, son of Robert. He was born in Boston in 1801, and was also brought up a merchant. He became the largest hardware dealer in the city of his birth and one of its leading citizens. Thus for four generations are combined commercial activity and success, business integrity and training, with patriotic devotion and exalted principle as a basis for effort to the ends of public welfare. With the reduction of the foreign trade and commercial interests of Boston by legal interferences, by non-intercourse and embargo, by the War of 1812, and subsequently by tariff restrictions of 1816 and following years,

5

with the shifting of the centres of business interest away from Boston and Philadelphia to New York— the port so situated as to command the trade with the interior—the ancestral line of Haskins breaks its New England allegiance. Thereafter it must be followed in Brooklyn and New York.

Waldo Emerson Haskins, father of the subject of this sketch, and son of Thomas Waldo, the Boston hardware merchant, was born in Roxbury, Massachusetts, in 1827. His mother was Mary Soren. After completing his education, in 1851, he removed to New York and engaged in banking with his uncle, George Soren. He then married Amelia Rowan Cammeyer, daughter of Charles Cammeyer, of New York. To them were born two children, Charles Waldo and Emma Parsons. Till 1884 Mr. Haskins's father lived to be his companion—to give him counsel and advice.

Charles Waldo Haskins, sixth of the American line, had back of him, therefore, the natural characters and inherited experience, the transmitted qualities of thought and the habits of life that patriotism and culture, high principle and noble activity may give. Such is the background of ancestral personality for our sketch.

A slightly higher light is given by his educational interests. Professor Haskins received his primary training in private schools. It being the intention of his parents that he should become a civil engineer, he subsequently entered the famous Polytechnic Institute of Brooklyn, where he graduated in 1867. There his academic record was such that the president predicted notable achievements for him as an engineer. The career of engineer, however, was not to his liking, and having come to the age of discretion—when personal decision was called for, when opinion was reflected from experience as well as from respect for the advice and judgment of elders—he turned to the field of Accountancy. As a preparation, the polytechnical school had given him a knowledge of many of the physical bases of business; drill in mathematics had laid the foundations for financial computation and financial record. A five years' apprenticeship in the accounting department of the old and well-known house of Frederick Butterfield & Company, in New York City, was his first school of experience. Afterwards nearly two years were spent in the schools of Paris. He then made a tour of Europe before returning to Wall Street, where he found a temporary connection with the banking and broking house of his father. Here he remained some time before setting out on his professional career.

Before this dimly perceived ancestral past and these somewhat more clearly outlined experiences of youth stands out the man. In this sketch it is not the purpose to bring out his many sides— his intellectual career and attainment, his high social qualities and broadly social bearing, his family and friendly ties, his large-hearted generosity—simply to portray him in his life work, and in this to suggest for what he stood. Entering the accounting department of the North River Construction Company (then building the New York, West Shore, and Buffalo Railway) his ability and training were soon recognized; he shortly was given supervision over the construction accounts of the North River Company. Upon the completion of the "West Shore," he was retained in the service of the railroad company as General Book-keeper and Auditor of Disbursements. This road was soon afterwards absorbed by the Vanderbilt system. It was then that he decided to open an office for general practice and enter on the profession of Public Accountancy. In the prosecution of his professional work he incidentally held several important administrative offices — among others, Secretary of the Manhattan Trust Company, Secretary of the Old Division Construction Company, Comptroller of the Central Georgia Railway, Comptroller of the Ocean Steamship Company, Comptroller of the Chesapeake and Western Railroad, Receiver of the Augusta Mining and Investment Company, etc. But it is in his attitude towards his profession—Independent Public Accountancy — that are found the lines of greatest strength. A study of this part of the portrait must prove of highest worth to those interested in his work.

Before proceeding with a study of leading characters, however, it may be well to call attention to another part of the background—that having direct contact with features of professional prominence. At the time Mr. Haskins left the banking and broking house of his father there was little in the field of Accountancy in the United States to make it attractive, little to encourage a young man of ambition and superior training. Then the accountant was not much above the level of clerk or office boy; in America he was little more than a book-keeper—following the conventional forms and methods that had grown up in small enterprise. Had Mr. Haskins's notion of Accounting come from this sort of contact, it is highly probable that he would never have chosen this for a professional career. Training abroad, however, had suggested the possibilities of a liberal profession. Contact with the many sides of financial life pointed to the need for higher Accountancy. With a serious purpose of doing what he might to raise American ideals to a higher plane, he entered the accounting department of the North River Construction Company. This gave first opportunity for development. Each engagement found new opportunity. Financial interests were being recast along broad lines; the old methods of accounting must be discarded; new methods must be introduced to give a base for sound discretion. No longer could the manager of enterprise come in direct contact with every detail of the business—for his information he must rely on his books and records of financial results. Mr. Haskins was inspired with the idea of reducing financial records to a scientific basis of classification and to be in a position to give professional advice to those who were made responsible for the safe conduct of large affairs. Not only was the need for better methods felt in private business, but the administrative departments of state were also becoming involved. The old systems of "book-keeping" had plainly failed to meet the demands of modern enterprise.

It was during a professional engagement with the Federal Government at Washington that Mr. Haskins was brought in contact with Mr. Elijah Watt Sells, a man somewhat his junior in years, but one who had won his way to prominence as a professional accountant in railway service in the Middle West. In 1893 Mr. Haskins and Mr. Sells were appointed as expert accountants under the Joint Commission of the Fifty-third Congress, to revise the accounting system of the National Government. This signal recognition of the professional ability of each served only as an introduction. As the work of revision progressed, each found that the methods and the high professional ideals of the other were in harmony with his own. Their mutual estimates were strengthened by expressions from those in high official position. Among the many published compliments which their successful labors evoked was one from Senator Redfield Proctor, of Vermont, who had spent much time with them in going over the details of their work. In the United States Senate he declared (July 15, 1894) that "these experts are men thoroughly competent, experienced, and skilful, and have been extremely careful and conservative in their methods." Having established confidence in their ability and in their thorough-going mastery of the subject in hand, their recommendations to the Joint Commission were adopted, and the new methods suggested were put into immediate operation. The improvement wrought has since been attested by all the accounting officers of the several departments. The system installed worked an annual saving of more than $600,000 in the expenses of administration, besides placing in the hands of administrators such summaries and data as vastly to improve the service. The expressed gratitude of the Commission may be added as further evidence of appreciation of the work accomplished. When the final Report was handed to the Commission, the following letter, bearing date March 2, 1895, was returned: "*Messrs. C. W. Haskins and E. W. Sells, Experts under the Joint*

Commission, etc.—GENTLEMEN,—In concluding the work of the Commission, it affords me special pleasure to express to you appreciation of the valuable services you have rendered. To your rare business capacity and peculiar adaptation to analyzing old and formulating plans for new methods in great measure is due the credit for the reorganization of the accounting system of the United States Government. It was, in many respects, the most extensive and important undertaking of the kind in the history of the country, and its success in expediting and simplifying the public business without removing any of the necessary safeguards has been fully demonstrated and attested by all the officials affected thereby. Very respectfully, (*Signed*) ALEX. M. DOCKERY, *Chairman Joint Commission.*"

The result of association in the work of "The Joint Commission of Congress to inquire into the status of Laws Organizing the Executive Departments" was a partnership alliance. In 1895 an office was opened in the Johnston Building, 30 Broad Street, New York, under the style of Haskins & Sells. This was but the beginning. Demand for professional accounting services grew so rapidly that over half a floor in this large downtown office building was finally required for the accommodation of New York engagements and for the administration of branch offices established in London, Chicago, St. Louis, and Pittsburg. In the organization of this professional service, quite as much as in the reorganization of the business of others, may be seen the constructive genius of the two men, for after 1895 their efforts were entirely co-operative. Each new accountant that came into working contact was either fitted into complementary relation or discarded, as he showed himself capable or incapable of adjustment to the professional standards set up. By this process of selection a working force was brought together; at the time of Mr. Haskins's death the co-operative group, which had begun in 1895 with Messrs. Haskins & Sells, had expanded to include forty principal accountants, besides about sixty assistant accountants and forty clerks. With such a co-ordinated force of professional men working in one group, it may be understood how it was possible in the year 1901–2 to undertake the reorganizing of the whole financial system of the city of Chicago, and to supervise the new system there installed, besides carrying on between two hundred and three hundred other large independent accounting operations.

Returning to the field of accounting as it was when Mr. Haskins entered it, we get a contrast unparalleled in the development of professional science. At that time the methods of the country store and of the small company were being carried down to modern undertaking through the book-keeper. The contrast between inherited book-keeping methods and professional Accountancy is illustrated in the results of the Chicago operation. A brief of accounting methods employed January 1, 1900, shows: (1) that there was a lack of uniformity and a confusion of methods inherited from the past which practically made the records of the city unavailable for administrative purposes; (2) that the accounts with different city departments, as shown on the books of the Comptroller, in many instances did not agree with the same accounts on the books kept by the departments; (3) that there was no adequate system of audit and no way of bringing the various accounts into harmony; (4) that the Comptroller lacked the authority in many instances to compel a uniform method and had not adequate power to inspect or audit before authorizing disbursement; (5) that there was such variety in the methods of disbursements as to make auditing and verification difficult, even if adequate authority were given; (6) that in the record of receipts and disbursements both ordinary and extraordinary receipts were accredited to the general funds and subsequently distributed, so that the general accounts in many instances did not furnish an intelligent statement of operating expense as distinct from construction and other permanent accounts; (7) that all warrants drawn on the Treasurer were paid by him by means of his own private check, and these were not a part of the public records; (8) that entries and changes in estimates of valuation were made against what was known as a "stock account," thus making statements of current revenues and expenses more uncertain; (9) that the special assessment books were frequently destroyed, thus leaving a large amount of trust funds without books of original entry; (10) that errors and discrepancies of account were adjusted by "posting" a balance without investigation of the errors or discrepancies; (11) that the item "cash," as shown in the general balance-sheets rendered, was stated without regard to the funds to which the cash belonged, thus giving a false impression as to available assets; (12) that there was no record of disbursements in the Comptroller's office, except the warrant record, and this was defective and lacking in detail; (13) that there was no record in the Comptroller's office of compensation in arrears, and no record of departmental materials and supplies; (14) that no proper record was kept of current or fixed liabilities of the city, and the city had no means of finding out the extent of its present indebtedness.

To get the other side of the picture, we turn to the current report of the Comptroller—made after the new system had been in operation one year. The features of the new systems, as there set forth, are as follows: "(1) Uniformity in accounting methods; (2) concentration of the accounting in the Comptroller's office; (3) collection of all revenue by the City Collector; (4) daily remittances; (5) monthly reports and balances between the Comptroller and all departments; (6) monthly financial report of the Comptroller; (7) organization of an Audit Bureau and of a methodical plan of auditing by officers and employés retained specially for that purpose and independent of all departments; (8) accruement of revenues on the General Books of the City, where they will always be evident as obligations due the city until paid; (9) approval of all contracts and requisitions for supplies by the Comptroller, to prevent departments from incurring liabilities in excess of appropriation; (10) the issuance of all fiscal stationery, forms, and receipts, consecutively numbered by the Comptroller, and holding the departments responsible for their use or cancellation; (11) the use of graduated stubs or coupon receipts to check the collection of money; (12) the establishment of a complete chain of accounting, from the inception of revenue or expense, throughout the various branches of the city, to the Comptroller's office, where all the accounting is finally centralized." As a result of the better administrative control effected, we learn that the revenues of the city, from direct and indirect taxation, fees of departments, etc., have increased nearly a million dollars, while the permanent saving expenses of the administration have been reduced over seventy thousand dollars per year.

No better evidence of the high professional character of Accountancy could be given than in the results of its application to the large affairs of to-day. It has taken a place by the side of Law. The old professions have been the product of slow growth. The cultures known as Theology, Medicine, and Law have required centuries to develop. Engineering, Dentistry, and some of the more modern professions have reached a plane of recognition more quickly, but the profession of Accountancy in two decades has risen from a place of almost menial service to one of the highest respect and honor. From the place of clerk and book-keeper, the accountant has come to take rank with those old and time-honored professions—and this as a necessary complement to modern financial and industrial progress.

It is in the development of the professional aspects of the field of accounting that Mr. Haskins's largest service has been rendered. Here it is that we find "what he stood for." The living profession stands as a monument on which may be found his name written in conspicuous letters. Mr. Haskins, throughout his busy life, was ever an advocate of "professional standards" in business employment; the essays and addresses here collected are among his literary contributions to this educational movement. On occasion when he was called to deliver himself before men interested in the advancement of business science, he was ever ready to respond. That Mr. Haskins was thoroughly in earnest in his effort to impress professional ideals upon his fellows, his whole life stands in evidence. No meeting of accountants was too remote to be reached by him; no Association of bankers, of business men, or of educators issued a call to him without generous response when it was within the range of possibility for him to be present. His enthusiasm and his leadership in the movement for legislation in the United States requiring State examinations for the title Certified Public Accountant (C. P. A.), his service as president of the first New York State Board of Examiners, his enterprise in the establishment of the first school to give a professional training in Accountancy, and his activities as first Dean of this School, all stand out and give force to his effort in the interest of winning for business a professional standing. As he looked out on the future he saw for the man of affairs—for the directors of those mighty interests which make for human welfare—a place in the hierarchy of learning as exalted as in the past has been assigned to the divine or to the man of letters, and to him this was not an idle dream, for he was among those who had climbed to eminence and was drawing others after him.

Legal recognition of the young profession, Public

Accountancy, was but the first step towards its establishment. Mr. Haskins recognized that the large body of American accountants must remain on a relatively low level unless some adequate provision were made for preliminary training. To this end much of his time was spent attending conferences and conventions of educators on this and cognate subjects. Finally, the Chancellor of New York University was interested in plans for installing a professional school of accounting as a part of the educational scheme of his institution, and on July 28, 1900, official approval of the Council was given to the enterprise. In planning its foundation, however, a much more ambitious venture was proposed, and to provide for the development of collateral professional training in business subjects the new department was given the name of the School of Commerce, Accounts, and Finance. Of this Mr. Haskins was made first Dean; in the organization of the faculty he accepted the Chair of Auditing and History of Accounting. His first aim was to bring together in the School such a corps of trained educators and practising accountants as would meet the educational requirements of the State Board of Examiners under the law of 1896. Later it was hoped that this line of specialization might be supplemented by the addition of still other groups of instruction till his plans for higher professional business education might be fully realized. In recognition of distinguished services in the cause of commercial education, New York University a year later conferred on Mr. Haskins the degree Master of Letters.

The more varied phases of Mr. Haskins's career may be shown by quotation and brief drawn from *Contemporary American Biography*. As a writer, Professor Haskins was lucid, scholarly, and convincing; his writings were original, and showed a wide acquaintance with the classics of the best European as well as British and American authors. Although occupied so fully with his professional work, much of which was of a private nature, Professor Haskins took a deep interest in public affairs. In this he was outspoken and active in support of good government, particularly of the City of New York. Besides his well-tested capacity and integrity, he was a man of great personal magnetism, kindly in disposition, cordial and hearty in his manner. Of stalwart physique, Professor Haskins had a decided taste for the "strenuous life." He had travelled widely in the United States and Europe, was a good linguist in French, German, and Italian, and, strange as it may seem, this devotee to figures and finance had a natural artistic taste, which was so well marked in youth that it led him to study Art under the best instructors in Europe. Several of his early productions, still preserved, show ability.

Besides being connected with the State and local Associations of Accountants, Professor Haskins was an Honorary Member of the Association of American Railway Accounting Officers of the United States; he took an active part in the organization of a number of patriotic societies, had been Treasurer-General of the National Society of the Sons of the American Revolution, and was Secretary-General of this Society at the time of his death; he was active and prominent in furthering the work of the National Municipal League and a member of its Committee on Uniform Municipal Accounting. He was also a member of the Society of the Mayflower Descendants, of the Society of Colonial Wars, and of the Military Order of Foreign Wars. The Manhattan Club, the Democratic Club, the Riding Club, the Country Club, the Westchester Club, and the New York Yacht Club were among his social club connections in his home city. He was also a member of the Metropolitan Club of Washington, D. C., and of the Piedmont Club of Atlanta, Georgia.

Professor Haskins was married in his thirty-third year to Miss Henrietta Havemeyer of the old and wealthy Havemeyer family of New York. Mrs. Haskins's father was Albert Havemeyer, a leading citizen and merchant. Her uncle was the Honorable William F. Havemeyer, twice Mayor of the city. Two daughters, Ruth and Noeline, share with Mrs. Haskins her bereavement.

II

BUSINESS TRAINING

THERE are two prejudices deeply rooted in the human breast which must be accounted for at the very threshold of the problem of business training. One is the prejudice against business as a calling or profession; the other is the prejudice against education. The prejudice against business as a pursuit has been fostered for untold ages by the traditions of the non-business classes, especially by the educated class. The prejudice against education, on the other hand, has been one of the most lively sentiments of the commercial community itself. The present movement in behalf of business training is making slow headway against the inertia of a great world-society bound together by hereditary ties, which in their inception and use were intended to resist educational progress. These prejudices, however, are doomed; they are dying, but they die hard.

PREJUDICES OF THE EDUCATED AGAINST BUSINESS

The prejudice against the pursuit of wealth is a bequeathment of antiquity; it is an inheritance from an age of social and political servility. A noted French writer, M. Courcelle Seneuil, thinks that the opinion of the ancients in this matter was founded at once upon an economic and a moral error. The moral error consisted in considering all commerce and industry as degrading and unworthy of the dignity of a freeman; the economic error consisted in believing that the grand total of wealth was not susceptible of augmentation or diminution. The first error was a logical sequence of the second. The Roman and the Greek philosophers, whose ideals were drawn from Sparta, considered the sum of worldly wealth as an almost invariable quantity. From this came the idea that any acquisition by an individual or a people was a loss to some other individual or people; by the philosophers of that time the acquisition of wealth was regarded as a kind of usurpation of a common patrimony.

While we consider such a philosophy erroneous, it has a history which not only explains its reasoning but also goes far to expose its fallacy when applied to present conditions. It speaks of a time when the people were divided into classes. The lowest stratum was made up of slaves. Above the slave in the social scale, but not above him in authority, was the client and the other members or attachés of the household. At the head of the stratified individual social group was the patriarch, who exercised control over persons and property within it. The tribe, the city, or the nation was considered as a still larger family—it was a self-centred, all - sufficient, kindred society, and acquisition was regarded as a group matter.

At that time business was looked upon as a matter of exchange between families or groups, in which it was taken for granted that any advantage gained by one group was necessarily at the expense of another. Acquisition by political groups was by war or by enforced tribute, and in this the same reasoning was applied. Thus the observation and conclusion based on the group ideals of the time gave a basis for the moral teaching which placed *acquisition* on a very low plane; in business it was based on cunning, while, *politically*, robbery and extortion were regarded as the underlying principle of all political operation. Those in control enriched themselves by a species of military brigandage approved by law and custom or by the prostitution of suffrages; those who held subordinate positions enjoyed privileges, a continuation of which required a certain obsequiousness of attitude towards the great. The pillaging conquests of Alexander, of Paulus Æmilius, of Mummius, were universally applauded; the extortions of Verres, of Sallust, and of many others were accepted by public opinion, and, if sometimes punished, it was rather under the influence of political rivalry than from a sentiment of public morality. Industry, on the other hand, was the calling of slaves, and was unworthy of serious contemplation by free-men. These rude ideas, slowly modified, have—through the activities of a professional teaching class, through social inertia, and through the maintenance of settled prejudice—worked their way down the ages.

To-day, however, all the errors upon which these prejudices repose have been exposed and denounced to the world. Religion has long proclaimed it the duty of every man to labor, and has declared industry an individual obligation and a social necessity. Political economy has proven that the sum of wealth existing in the world is susceptible of increase and diminution, that it is increased by industry, and that, consequently, every man may enrich himself without impoverishing his fellows. It has gone further, and proved that it is impossible for an individual to become rich by legitimate means without enriching the other members of the society in which he moves. Property rights have come to be grounded upon industrial activity rather than upon conquest or mere possession. We are in a fair way to break the last link of this chain of ancient servility. We are learning that the pursuit of wealth by means of industry is an occupation quite as ennobling and may be based on a culture as "liberal" as any other. Socially, the seeker after riches obligates himself to satisfy the needs of his fellows and to augment the collective power of his nation; religiously, he fulfils an obligation; morally, he opposes idleness, that mother of all vice, and worthily adds his own contribution to the public welfare. Who can do more? To-day what man dare say that, by virtue of his occupation or profession, he is morally superior to a laborer or an active business man?

But again let us consider the problem of wealth from the individual point of view. What is wealth or fortune? It is an aggregate of things useful that has been acquired by an individual. As the possessor and proprietor of useful things, the individual who devotes himself to their acquisition becomes a more useful man. Wealth gives to the individual the power still further to multiply or to produce things useful to himself or to others and thus to increase the sum total of "goods." Through voluntary co-operation, based on consent and peaceful exchange of goods and services, wealth places at the disposal of the individual possessing it a certain amount of natural force and human service —a power which, like all other powers, may be used well or ill, but which in itself is an increase of opportunity and therefore a good. The possession of wealth is doubtless an occasion and a means of evil-doing—of satisfying the pride and other vices of him who possesses it; it is also an occasion and a means of well-doing—of satisfying the most no-ble, the most charitable inspirations of the soul.

Morals and religion, when to-day they teach a contempt of money, are not to be understood as prescribing a neglect of it or an abstinence from effort necessary to its acquisition. For how, then, could we reconcile their precepts with the funda-mental principle which constituted industry the first obligation of man? In teaching this contempt of wealth, religion and morals forbid the entire at-tachment of the mind thereto. Because money is perishable and of short duration—as are all the useful things of this world, and as are we ourselves who enjoy them—morals and religion tell us that wealth is not the end of human life and activity. We are taught that the chief thing is our attitude towards our brother; that our final interest should be one of social welfare, of humanity; and that riches are the means of fulfilling our obligations, of satisfying the eternal laws of "humanity" by which we are to be regulated and governed. And, truly, wealth ought not to be the one end of life, nor even its chief end—only the means to be employed tow-ards an end. But since it is the necessary means, the pursuit and employment of it are always and everywhere the legitimate object of the greater part of human activity, and are closely related to the accomplishment of our most sacred duties.

But if riches is not the chief end of man, neither

can we pretend to have found this end in science, nor in poetry, nor in eloquence, nor in the fine arts, nor in the exercise of political duty. If we compare business or the industrial effort to gain an increase in useful things with all these other occupations, we find it neither less noble nor less honest nor less conformed to justice and morality. We may add, also, that it is not more egotistic, not a whit more selfish, and, as an expression of effort for common ends, it is within the reach of a greater number of intelligences, because, in the free organization of business, the talents of each individual interested in an enterprise are imperceptibly drawn into the current of the common good, while he himself is laboring might and main to satisfy his own ambition.

The pursuit of riches, then, by means of commercial enterprise, is not to be disdained, and the function of the business man is not to be looked upon as beneath other social functions. The man of affairs has need for as much intelligence, as much force of mind, as much character, as much judgment as he who follows another profession. One of the benefits already accruing to society from this new educational movement is that we are learning to reserve for the business man the place in public estimation which rightfully belongs to him—that we are ceasing to sacrifice him in our esteem to those who exercise the so-called "liberal" professions. The prejudice which has existed in favor of these professions has long drawn to them the most persistent educational effort and the most ardent ambition, to the vast detriment of the industrial welfare of the world.

PREJUDICE OF BUSINESS MEN AGAINST EDUCATION

Having considered the traditional prejudice against the pursuit of business as a calling or profession, let us now turn to the prejudice against education—a prejudice for which, as we have said, the commercial community is in large measure responsible. This prejudice against instruction—also an old and powerful one—is rarely expressed in words, and is in some sense hidden, but it shows itself continually in sentiment and action. True, it is gradually losing its force, but we must recognize the fact that it still exists and is widely spread.

Every prejudice has a cause. A collective opinion cannot be established and become paramount unless at the time of its establishment it be in some respects true. It must contain at least a modicum of truth, and it is necessary that we seek this out that we may know the quantum of error. Opinion, in this respect, is a gold-bearing mineral; it must be analyzed and reduced. Under the name "liberal" instruction we usually designate the matter of our primary and secondary teaching — viz., reading, writing, geography, mathematics, ancient languages, history, physical and natural sciences, and the fine arts. Those who excel in any one branch of knowledge are known as scholars or *savants*. Then we say: "A scholar, a *savant*, is of little force in business; scholarship makes a man incapable of active participation in the affairs of business life."

If we go back to the origin of opinions of this kind we find them established as a sort of reaction against absolute and opposed opinions. When in the course of human events there was no longer a privileged nobility whose glory consisted in not being able to sign its own name, literary instruction became a sort of distinction to those who enjoyed its benefits, and, as a consequence of this distinction, it often inspired them with a ridiculous presumption. Scholars allowed themselves to believe that being possessed of this instruction, to which the world and even society seemed to attach so great an importance, by this fact alone they were constituted personages fit to govern all things. This presumption, sustained by common opinion, was in itself a powerful cause of incapacity.

So-called "cultural" instruction has but few applications in matters of business. He who possesses it in the highest degree does not find therein the elements essential to the humblest business enterprise, and if he on this account imagines himself capable of conducting business affairs he must necessarily fail. As well seek to train a physician, a lawyer, a civil engineer, or a dentist without instruction especially adapted to his calling. The trouble has been that the so-called "cultural" studies are those which were originally adapted to the training of men for the ministry and for literary calling. The old-time Latin-Greek course is itself a highly specialized training to this end. Nothing could be more fallacious than the position taken that this is a *liberal* training—nothing more futile than to attempt to fit one for medical practice or for business by giving one the training intended for specialization in the ministry. If one wishes or has the opportunity to take both, well and good; each will add something to the store of knowledge. But as well expect one to be able to take a position as resident physician in a hospital after training in the dissection of Greek verbs as to command a place in a business house.

The peculiar elation given to one so trained, by reason of the prevailing presumption among the devotees of so-called "culture," stands in the way of success. Placed in a subordinate position, the possessor of such an education performs his work grudgingly, believing himself capable of better things because, forsooth, he is a scholar. He is self-deceived, and his very presumption strikes him with further incapacity. His attitude might be likened to that of a day laborer who, because he can read and write, thinks that he may therefore claim a clerical position. With a minimum of instruction as a basis, one may go on and learn much; but the instruction itself, either minimum or maximum, does not constitute a man's title to any particular place in the business world.

BENEFITS OF EDUCATION IN BUSINESS

But, presumption aside—which, even sustained by an error of opinion, is detestable—what, with reference to real aptitude for business, are the benefits of academic instruction? We answer that he who has it in its lowest degree may better understand his work than he who has it not. The very beginning of culture opens his intelligence and gives him the means of acquiring further knowledge. However poor may be the literature of his trade or profession, such books as do exist he may read. In industrial pursuit he has bodily activity to give physical development and vigor. By substituting literary recreation for grosser pleasure, he may become a better tradesman or merchant and a better man.

So, in fuller measure, with the young man possessed of a good, solid, higher education. His study of language has been an intellectual exercise which has developed the faculties of his mind—

more than this, it enables him to read business experience from other tongues. His notion of the elements of the sciences preserves him from gross errors as to the world of fact, and, better still, will enable him to apply his powers of thought to the making of better business judgments in all relations where such scientific knowledge is required. But while he will comprehend more quickly than his unlettered brother, here his advantage will find a limit — it may, in a measure, be offset by his inferiority in other respects. For example, he may not yet have acquired the habits which are so important to the man of affairs. Skill in any particular calling depends largely on acquiring habits which give efficiency. He may not be possessed of a knowledge of essential technical facts which are to be learned only by practical experience. If he misunderstands this truth he is the loser. If, however, knowing that he does not know, and being determined to learn, he sets himself to the study of affairs by scientific inquiry and practice, he will succeed more readily than the young man without education. Nothing short of too much presumption and too little judgment, the sign of both of which is vanity, can hinder his success.

As for the man whose life-specialty has been letters or philosophy—he who has acquired culture, habits, and training for this form of product—as for the philosopher, his inaptitude for the conduct of affairs will readily be admitted. Especially is this true if he has arrived at a time of life in which habits are neither acquired nor lost—when he neither learns nor forgets. The sciences proceed from particular facts to general conclusions. *A priori* reasoning serves simply as a guide to further research; scientific conclusion is established synthetically— *i.e.*, by so associating the known facts as to make the conclusion imperative. In the life of the business man, general conclusions are reached largely from experience. These conclusions are the means by which he foresees practical results and often contrives adaptations to ends. The facts with which the scientist is engaged may be taken from a restricted field of inquiry for the purpose of establishing a special science. If within the field of business, if his conclusions are useful to the man of affairs, he may at once become of valued service; he may, however, become a trained specialist in a line quite foreign to a business specialty. The manager of enterprise may be engaged in a field which has to do with the combination of an infinity of composite forces, human and material, entirely outside of the experience and training of the philosopher or scientist. A long habit of scientific labor outside the field of business may, therefore, be taken as presumptive evidence of unfitness for commercial affairs.

The results of this lack of harmony of interests

34

between most men of letters (philosophers and scientists), on the one hand, and men of business (men who have received their "special" training entirely outside of the schools), on the other, are twofold: (1) The "schools" have so far shown little or no scientific interest in the field of business. The only kind of academic training which pretends to correspond to this interest is Economics. Most of the writings of this nature, however, have been on Political Economy—a body of abstractions formulated by persons almost wholly without scientific training or business experience—a body of deductions from considerations of public welfare. We are, therefore, without a trained staff of teachers capable of giving specialized instruction in business sciences. (2) The business man, finding his problem an entirely different one, being ignored by one class, and finding the only school of academicians that professes an interest in his field ignorant of the facts, comes to treat business education with contempt.

Professor Herrick, director of the Commercial course in the Central High-School of Philadelphia, writing of this condition of affairs, says: "Business men, on the one hand, pride themselves on their ability to get on without education, thinking success to be a matter of smartness rather than of training; and not infrequently do we find men contrasting their business success with their limited education and boasting that education is not an essential for

35

success. Over against this is the cordial spurning of the practical that not infrequently characterizes educators. An instrument of education that has utility is felt by them to be contaminated. Men in school and college are not unlike that Cambridge professor of mathematics who concluded a brilliant demonstration in his chosen subject with the statement: 'Gentlemen, the most beautiful thing about that proof is that it can never be of any practical value to any living being.' As schoolmen we are too prone to feel that if a subject of study has practical value it is besmirched. The problem of making our education practical, and that without too great sacrifice of the ends of training, is not of easy solution, yet it is this problem with which commercial education is confronted. The only hope of success is in having men of affairs and educators come to a better agreement as to what education is and how subjects having a practical value can be utilized in obtaining it."

The new so-called higher commercial education movement is intended to bridge over the chasm between study and business—between the scholar, the savant, the recluse, if you will, on the one hand, and the sturdy, quick-witted man of action, the handler of the material products of the world, the money-maker, if you will, on the other. It recognizes the utility of education, and seeks to adapt instruction to the exigencies of making a living for society; and it recognizes the utility of practical information, and seeks to render this information available to the student before he shall have been thrown out into the maelstrom of business experience.

But let it be remembered that no school, no theory can take the student into the innermost heart of affairs. They can give him all the information that can be collected, organized, and digested by those who become trained specialists in this form of scientific research. In so far as knowledge of the facts and relations or the institutions and agencies of business can be reduced to scientific order and conclusion, general business instruction comes to be of the highest value, both for its disciplinary use and for its subject matter. Absolute contact, however, with real business is indispensable; it is very imprudent to enter upon the career of business management without having first had some experience as an apprentice. The habits, the customs, even the language of a business are transmitted by tradition and mutual instruction—often without the teacher or the learner suspecting that he is imparting or receiving instruction. The old apprenticeship system is almost a thing of the past, and the new school of commerce is almost a thing of the future. Under present conditions it would seem that the future leader of affairs may best combine the advantages of study and experience by passing a year or two in a subordinate position in the line of business he intends to follow. Studying under professional teachers may well be arranged to apportion the time between study and practice. If such training may be arranged, science and practice should each supplement the other.

The characteristic feature of all professional education is that it has a determined and well-defined end in view — theological education, to educate for the ministry; medical education, to give us our physicians; legal education, to train our lawyers. In the same sense commercial education should raise up a trained class of *entrepreneurs*. Professor Ely, of the University of Wisconsin, writing of the organization of business, has well explained the necessity for the adoption of this French word and for the present extension of its meaning. "The one who manages business for himself," he says, "was formerly called an undertaker or an adventurer; but the first word has been appropriated by one small class of business men, and the latter has acquired a new meaning, carrying with it the implication of rashness and even of dishonesty. We have consequently been obliged to resort to the French language for a word to designate the person who organizes and directs the productive

38

factors, and we call such a one an *entrepreneur*. The function of the *entrepreneur* has become one of the most important in modern economic society. He has been well called a captain of industry, for he commands the industrial forces, and upon him, more than any one else, rests the responsibility for success or failure. A business which has achieved magnificent success often becomes bankrupt when, owing to death or other cause, an unfortunate change in the *entrepreneur* is made. The prosperity of an entire town has sometimes been observed to depend upon half a dozen shrewd captains of industry. It may be said, then, that the large reward these often receive is only a legitimate return for splendid social services. Such is the case, provided this reward is gained honestly and without oppression. Sometimes gains are partially legitimate and partially illegitimate. It is this mixture, observed by all in notorious cases, which has probably led more than anything else to indiscriminate attacks on the profits of the captains of industry. The productivity of industry depends largely upon the harmonious development of all the factors. Sometimes labor is especially needed, sometimes capital, sometimes land; most frequently what is needed above everything is a better organization of productive factors. Organization is often defective, and talent for organization and management is unfortunately rare."

39

This talent for organization and management, described by Professor Ely as "unfortunately rare," is the distinguishing feature of the *entrepreneur*, whose office, in the conduct of modern affairs, is more often than otherwise a delegated one. His *profession* consists in conceiving and conducting business enterprises, or some one enterprise to which he is devoted, or some department of an enterprise, which department may have within itself the essential elements of a distinctive individual enterprise. The *entrepreneur*, as a specialist, is the administrator of the world's business; wherever business is conducted, he is the conductor, and whatever the nature of his business, or however small or great its magnitude, he will succeed or fail according as he applies or fails to apply thereto certain well-defined principles of thought and action.

"The importance of the directive function in business," says the distinguished economist, M. Leroy - Beaulieu, "is proved by all the facts of experience. The success or failure of an enterprise is determined by its administration. Put forty thousand recruits under the command of a Hannibal, and he will gain twenty battles; give sixty thousand veterans to a Varro, and they will be cut to pieces. And so," he continues, "it is in business; the capacity of the commercial class enriches a locality or a nation; its incapacity is its ruin." If schools of training are of advantage in the preparation of a military administration—if a corps of scientific instructors can add to the efficiency of a military general, the same reasoning would lead us to conclude that men who are to take charge of the great armies of workers on which our industrial welfare and success depend may also direct the forces under them to better effect if we have schools competent to give this kind of instruction.

THE DEMAND FOR PROFESSIONAL TRAINING

To meet the demand, then, of the modern business world for an adequate supply of trained business men—now so "unfortunately rare"—is the object of the present missionary movement in the interest of better facilities for business education. This movement recognizes, in business training, two teaching elements: the school and "the school of the world," or experience. A physician is not made in the school; his education goes on after he has entered upon his "practice." But the practical wisdom, the scientific conclusions of the profession having been gathered up, these, through a corps of trained instructors, are instilled into the mind of the student while in the medical school, and he is thereby the better able to begin his work as a practitioner. So of the business man.

He may not be made in the school, nor in the world of business, but the practical knowledge and wisdom of the business world having been gathered, formulated, and imparted to him in a professional school, he should emerge armed with economic truth and information, the better able to begin his struggle in the battle of life.

The question of pedagogy, as related to business, is: How much of this economic knowledge and wisdom can be brought into the school and properly assimilated, and in what relative proportions, to the best advantage? Answering this question in a general way, it may be said that all of the information concerning business that can be brought together into a classified science may there be made available as a basis for training; and in this respect the work is not yet begun. The field only awaits trained research to gather in large sheaves of information by which the business man himself may profit, to say nothing of the youth seeking preparation. Leaving this question, however, for time to answer—and time alone can answer it—let us turn our attention to the subject-matter of business education. This subject-matter we shall endeavor to view, as we have already indicated, from the standpoint of the practical, or, as we may say, the "professional" administrator; that is, we shall not confine ourselves to a discussion of mere clerical requirements, nor, on the other hand, shall we extend our survey over the broad field of scientific economics and the still wider field of social science.

THE SPECIAL TRAINING REQUIRED FOR THE MANAGER

The industrial enterprises of the world, differing technically in a thousand ways, exhibit to the trained mind some common characters in that (1) they all must have capital and material equipment; (2) they all require co-operation in the productive activities—*i.e.*, operation; (3) they all must find a market for their product or service at a price which will yield a profit. The several branches of instruction available to one who is seeking special training for business management may be discussed with reference to these common characters.

Problems of capitalization lie at the very threshold of management. On this depends the ability of the *entrepreneur* to obtain the physical and financial equipment necessary to successful operation. The problems of capitalization, however, must always bear a direct relation to operation. In management, the details are all reducible to the relation of profits—*i.e.*, net return to proprietors—to capitalization. The object of business is financial gain. I say financial gain because a gain or a loss on the "assets" or properties of persons, acquired through business, is always interpreted in

43

the language of Finance. The judgment of valuation (greater or less worth) of "assets" at any particular time is always expressed by reference to a monetary standard as a means of reducing the result to a common denominator. All those who conceive and direct industrial and commerical enterprises have the same end in view—namely, to augment their fortunes. They accomplish this end by the same means—*i.e.*, all business in its results may be reduced to the rendering of service to others; these services, or the objects in which they are incorporated, are exchanged in such manner that each party "gains" thereby. The motive which animates one to serve another is that by so doing he may the better accomplish his own end. The end is net profit. The incentive to the handling of labor and capital is the production of an income in excess of expense and loss; on this necessarily hangs the interest of the *entrepreneur* in all economic questions entering into the conduct of his business; the enterprise must "pay" or it will go to the wall.

The financial interest, therefore, runs through every department and activity of business, from capitalization to final distribution in the form of dividends. Instruction in Finance should first be sought by one desiring special training for business management. One about to enter on a business career should avail himself of the best scientific knowledge obtainable, to fit him to make financial judgments. He should know the various forms of funds available and the advantages of each, understand instruments of transfer of credit funds, how funds are obtained, and the instruments and institutions employed. He should understand methods of capitalization and the relative advantages of each method from the point of view of his own business purpose; he should know the financial arrangements to be made for equipment, keeping in mind the length of time involved in acquiring physical equipment and the capital chafges incident thereto; he should appreciate the financial relations of operation, looking towards profits. Should the *entrepreneur* be called upon to administer a brankrupt estate, he should know the methods incident thereto—likewise the advantages to be gained by the several methods of reorganization as a means of adjusting capitalization to net earnings and net profits. Problems of consolidation and agreements based on community of interest likewise have methods and advantages to be considered. All these furnish a basis for scientific financial education.

The physical equipment of enterprise furnishes another scientific field for instruction. This lies partly in the domain of engineering science, partly in the field of economic science. The problem is one of applying means to an end—of considering the advantages to the several kinds of equipment when applied to a definite service to be rendered. It further involves considerations of internal arrangement and adjustment for greatest economy of power and labor. It also involves a knowledge of markets and materials, of transportation facilities as well as of the location of available power and labor. So much for scientific instruction with respect to capitalization and equipment. The data of this field of inquiry are found not alone in Finance, but also in Engineering, Mechanics, and Architecture.

Turning to the second category above set forth (operation), we again find possibilities for scientific instruction preparatory to business. First among the subjects of specialized training to this end is Accountancy. While the business manager may expect to have some one to keep his financial records for him, he should have a knowledge of the essentials as an element in successful direction. It has before been observed that business success or failure resolves itself into an equation of earnings and expense finding a final net result in profit; and a second equation between net profits and proprietary capitalization finding a final net result in dividends. All business judgments of valuation, and all business contracts involving price, must be made with reference to these financial equations. Every judgment, therefore, pertaining to operation as well as to capitalization is measured by the final test of financial summaries shown in the accounts. The financial records or accounts of a business concern furnish the data from which proceed judgments as to operation and into which every business transaction resolves itself for a new basis for judgment. It is in accounts that experience is finally recorded; it is by the accounts that the service of the manager is in the end judged. Accounting has established in itself a literature which lends to the schools a foundation for scientific instruction.

The second problem within the field of operation is that of "industrial processes." The student inquirer should have at least an elementary knowledge of these. Such knowledge would fit him for more mature and more effective judgments as to the business or financial advantages to be gained from the one or the other process as applied to the specific problem that comes to him for solution. By such training he will be the more resourceful and the better armed for the service on which he has entered. While in this branch little is available to the student, the subject is one which is possessed of possibilities as large as the present scientific literary base.

Again, a knowledge of industrial organization lends itself to student inquiry. The centre of interest around which the data or organization are to be grouped and co-ordinated is working efficiency. In this the problem of labor and the most effective use of the services of others are involved. Questions of copartnership, of corporate control, and of directive responsibility, questions of division of labor and of industrial or commercial activities for best return at a given expense in salary and wage, all of these considerations properly belong to the larger subject—industrial organization. It is a social-industrial problem, and how many important life - problems are here involved may be dimly appreciated by the conscientious educator. On the moral side, old systems of training and thought too often have overlooked business activity. In fact, those systems of philosophy which regarded business and the acquisition of wealth as low and immoral *per se* must be entirely abandoned before any proper appreciation of this interest may be had. A morality of social-industrial organization should be taught, which will harmonize with the principles of honesty, integrity, and industry. It is a system of morals based on social economy and welfare, but still in harmony with the problem of industrial activity in business—activity directed towards individual gain; this must form the basis for new rules of business under conditions of broader organization. In the present initial stage of the new educational movement, this is the opportunity of our educational institutions for moral instruction. As teachers of morals, our professional educators may lift a noble standard and endue our

48

youth with manly strength to keep that standard out of the mud in the battle of life.

In the social-industrial relation, from purely selfish consideration, an elementary knowledge of hygiene may not be out of place. The administrator of a business enterprise must not only know how to employ his own vitality—he is to acquire a product in value greater than the sum of his expenses, this excess to cover losses as well as to include profits; to this end he must utilize all the productive forces at his command. Of these forces the chief and most important are within himself, but he must preserve his social forces from impairment as well as his mechanical plant and power. Professor Francis Walker, writing of the employing class in the modern stage of industrial development, says: "The laborer no longer looks to the employer to furnish merely food and tools and materials, but to furnish, also, technical skill, commercial knowledge, and powers of administration, to assume responsibilities and provide against contingencies, to shape and direct production, and to organize and control the industrial machinery. So important and difficult are these duties, so rare are the abilities they demand, that he who can discharge them will generally find the capital required. If he be the man to conduct business, food, tools, and materials will not, under our modern system of credit, long be wanting to him. On the other hand, without these higher qualifications, the mere possessor of capital will employ labor at the risk, almost the certainty, of total or partial loss. The employer, the *entrepreneur*, thus rises to be the master of the situation. It is no longer true that a man becomes the employer of labor because he is a capitalist. Men command capital because they have the qualifications to employ labor. To men so endowed, capital and labor alike resort for the opportunity to perform their several functions and to entitle themselves to share in the product of industry. By this is not meant that the employer is not, in any case, or to any extent, a capitalist, but that he is not an employer to the extent only to which he is a capitalist, nor is he an employer at all because he is a capitalist."

Here again, then, is the opportunity for the educator. The "master of the situation" here pictured by Professor Walker is the man of intellect. In the personal labor of the humblest *entrepreneur* the intellectual and moral will dominate the material element, and this will be more and more apparent as the enterprises to be conducted are of greater magnitude. The province of the higher business education is to put the moral and intellectual powers of our future administrators of affairs in the way of their highest development, and to give to these powers an inclination in the direction that must be followed in the activities of business life. It must be confessed, however, that pedagogy enters this field seriously handicapped with a weight of prejudice which must be shaken off, with a density of inexperience which practice alone can relieve, with a deplorable want of scientific knowledge which only hard study can supply. For long ages our men of commerce and industry have been left to battle their way to success with little more than a guerilla knowledge of the warfare of life, and now that modern conditions imperatively demand a new education, we are confronted with the somewhat humorously serious situation of an active set of men who know but cannot teach and a philosophical class who could teach but do not know. The teacher, therefore, must become a scientific inquirer into the field of human interest as well as a philosopher. He must gather up the wisdom of the world, not alone from *Poor Richard's Almanac*, but from many thousands of contemporaneous modest men of action; he must formulate, under the constant check of these men of concrete information, a "science of administration," and he must instil the principles of this science into the very life of the future *entrepreneur*. When we come to consider the employment of capital, we find that we are not yet free of the personality of the *entrepreneur*. His business will in many ways be a reflection of his character; he will use money well or ill as an administrator, about as he uses it as an individual, and in both capacities he will retain the habits acquired in his student days. In this consideration the teacher finds his enormous responsibility for the future of human welfare. Principles and habits of life and thought that are safe with your boy are safe with your man, safe with the individual, are safe in the hands of the administrator. Mill and other political economists have told us much of the "economic man" in the abstract, but here he is in the concrete. If in the past too little attention has been given to holding the student to a strict account, something may here be learned from the world of business and imparted to the life of the student.

A knowledge of the use of credit and of the responsibilities that go along with its use is essential to the manager. On the one hand, interest and discount are items of expense to be set off against earnings. Again, the employment of the capital obtained from others on contracts of credit, is subject to general rules and to certain moral considerations. There are certain special considerations concerning this use of credit upon which the man of affairs ought to have well-founded ideas, because there is no point from which errors and illusions are more likely to arise, and which are at the same time more dangerous. It is of the first importance that the student be morally and intellectually armed against the evils incident to the credit system—

that he be warned of the temptations which will beset him as a financial manager, so that he may enter the field of commerce as wary on the one hand as he is bold on the other. Fraud and embezzlement are often the unhappy sequel of mere prodigality in the outlay of capital obtained on contracts of future delivery, when it becomes apparent that the one who has so obligated himself must fail. "Our entire land," says Professor Ely, "is strewn with the ruins of businesses wrecked by men who have mismanaged the property which unwise credit gave into their hands."

While the employment of labor, as we have seen, is to the *entrepreneur* an expense of capital, this expense differs so widely from all other expenses, and plays so important a part in every enterprise, that in the constitution and conduct of a business it becomes a separate study. And this study must be pursued, apart from the claims of benevolence, upon strictly business grounds. The ever-living question before the employer—a question that must be heard, studied, and answered without vagueness— is how to obtain from the capital expended the greatest efficiency of labor. Here, then, the labor question takes its place as a part of the study of administration, and its connection with morals and religion on the one hand, and with scientific economics on the other, must be determined by necessity and not by sentiment.

The administrator of affairs, as we have seen, must be both a financier and an employer, and must be, under modern conditions, an educated man in both of these characters. A third requisite to good administration, partly dependent upon these two, is a well-grounded knowledge of the laws of association and of the contracts of society. He represents the co-operation of capital and labor; he brings them into intimate relations and imparts to them a common interest; he assumes their direction and takes upon himself their separate risks, covering the capitalist on the one hand and the employé on the other with the mantle of his own responsibility. But he is not free to exercise this responsibility except under certain restrictions. However great may be the society or company whose affairs he directs, he is but a member of society in the larger sense, of which society the capitalist and the employé are also members. In this more general sense society intervenes in the functions of the *entrepreneur* and limits his spontaneity of action. The importance of this condition of things, together with the errors and prejudices to which it gives rise, demands of the modern leader of business affairs a knowledge, not only of the natural laws of association, but of the legislation limiting the constitution and administration of commercial societies.

These are the general branches of knowledge

having to do with the constitution and organization of a business enterprise in which our educators may render service. The third general discussion of business training has to do with exterior relations of commercial venture; they are commonly grouped under five heads, already more or less familiar in our higher institutions of learning, and happily assuming a more practical aspect in their handling, as business men are being drawn into the agitation for sound business education. These are (1) economic and commercial geography as a means of knowing the location of materials and resources, as well as of markets and trade routes; (2) commerce, including the mechanism and organization of trade, methods of purchase and sale, advertising, etc.; (3) the laws governing exchange, including the economic basis for considerations of value—the consideration which is essential to every contract of exchange; (4) transportation, including the organization and mechanism of land and water carriage of goods and passengers, together with shipping devices and technique; (5) commercial crises, as affecting the return in profits through price fluctuations, the shifting of market demands, and the influence of these varying phenomena on ability to meet credit obligations incurred in the course of exchange.

ACADEMIC TRAINING TO BE SUPPLEMENTED BY PRACTICE

In the three fields of business interest above described there has already been developed a scientific literature such as may occupy the attention of the student, and which may give a proper base for scientific academic instruction which may go far towards placing business management on a professional footing. In some of our higher institutions of learning this training extends over three or four years. But when we come to the field of business practice, we find ourselves in a realm of education in which, at first blush, all grades, even down to the primary ones, seem to belong to the world of activity and experience. In these the question will be how far a school can admit the technique of business and yet be a school; how far the camel can be allowed to warm his nose without the master having to leave the tent. Polytechnical schools, however, have succeeded in the plastic and mechanical arts; why not in business? In agriculture and horticulture we have already developed the practice to a high level through government experimental stations. The technical school has much of practical training that pertains directly to business. In the so-called "Business College" the technique of trade and finance has been developed along lines such as will serve as preparation for

56

a clerk or a book-keeper. For higher technical training this side of business holds possibilities which await only the tardy process of bringing together the information and mechanism necessary to experimentation and practical drill. While the practice side is limited by its very nature, it still holds opportunity for further development.

One closing consideration. The subject of business training, as we are coming to view it, is of boundless extent; it opens up, as it were, a new world of education. It is capable of infinite subdivision, and will employ in its exploration and settlement the best efforts of "many men of many minds." I have endeavored in this essay to view the matter only in the light of administration; that is, of the *entrepreneur*, partly because this aspect of business training would have the interest of novelty to some, but especially because this is the nail that must be hit on the head sooner or later. I have not, therefore, taken account of the hundred and one accessories to business which of themselves are more or less important branches of education. Nor have I allowed for the fact that the business world is full of valuable men who are not administrators; these find their places, according to their tastes and natural talents, in some recognized position in touch with their leaders. Rising from rank to rank, as officers in an army, they may succeed the older generation as veterans fit for the supreme command. Professional business education, however, will be the same; that is, it will be, not how to read Sanskrit, but how to run a business enterprise. Again, we must not forget that not all directors of affairs are at the head of our gigantic combinations of industry, but that equally with these great generals, and with the merchant prince and the "Napoleon of Finance," the humblest conductor of a modest retail establishment, or manufactory, or private bank is an *entrepreneur*. To him, under modern conditions, a well-grounded business education is also becoming a *sine qua non*.

III

THE SCOPE OF BANKING EDUCATION

THE employments devoted to culture have been grouped under Religion, Morality, Philosophy, Art, Science, and Pedagogy. If we consider Religion and Morals as a part of Philosophy, and Art as applied Science, we have but three of these categories remaining—viz., Philosophy and Science (two distinct forms of acquiring knowledge), and Pedagogy (the philosophy, science, or art of imparting it). Prominent among the activities of mankind which are subjects of distinct consideration are Banking and Accountancy. I mention these two professions because, as a distinguished advocate of economic education has pointed out, Accountancy and Banking are first among the processes and methods of conducting business which in the development of American mercantile practice "have assumed stable forms." These two fields of specialized activity have come to be clearly marked out; within each has been developed a distinct interest.

I think that it will be conceded without argument that banking education has in mind the training for a calling or profession of men who are not yet prepared to engage actively in the work. Any consideration of "the scope of banking education" is, therefore, necessarily confronted by two problems: First, what amount of exact knowledge may be or already has been acquired on this subject? second, what instruments or methods now are, or may be, employed for imparting this knowledge outside of the bank itself?

Answering the first question, it must be conceded that the economic literature of the past leaves much to be desired. In its larger aspects it has been the result of the application of the methods of an antique philosophy and not of modern science. Philosophy in its logical processes is deductive; its method is not one of research; it assumes that a satisfactory body of knowledge has already been acquired for its premises; it proceeds to reason from conclusions already accepted, and from accepted conclusions it goes to still wider generalizations. Following this method, "political" economists have sought to enlighten the world as to the manner in which banking contributes to general welfare, as to the functions of exchange, theories of national and international trade, the influence of importations of gold in settlement of international balances, etc. All these are higher generalizations that proceed from the assumptions of a concrete knowledge of banking. This concrete knowledge, however, they do not possess. It is the very subject-matter of the training that should be given prior to making broader generalization, and which the banker recognizes as necessary before any reliable judgments may be formed on the subject.

This lack of exact knowledge about the subject, for purposes of instruction, has made some people sceptical as to the possibilities of giving in the schools a professional basis for banking. One who would look fairly upon the subject in hand must admit that there is still much to be learned before we can assure ourselves of any well-founded conclusions as a basis for sound thinking, within the schools, on the broader and wider financial relations. While a lack of educational literature may stand as an obstacle in the way of highest professional attainment, still we need not give ourselves over to educational despair. We already have made a considerable beginning. The subject is one that lends itself to research, and investigators trained to scientific methods of research are applying themselves to the task. No one will seriously contend that the data of the business are so far beyond the reach of scientific inquiry that the facts may not be collected, classified, and co-ordinated as a basis for education and for sound conclusion. If at present there is any lack of scientific literature on the subject, which would cause one to fall short of professional training in this field of specialization, it remains only to establish here a distinct professional interest to call workers to the harvest.

The development of a body of trained scientists, outside of the business of banking, will have a wide influence for good to the banker as well as to the business world at large. Banking, in its growth from unrecognizable beginnings to its present colossal proportions, has adopted or invented one improvement after another, but is still confessedly and dangerously behind the times. In support of this conclusion we have the statements of many of the most enlightened and prominent bankers of to-day. Former Secretary Gage expresses his thought in language as follows: "It is a strange anomaly that while in nearly every other department of life improvement is the indispensable rule, in the field of banking, finance, and exchange we go on with an indifferent regard to the handicap imposed by defective methods." In nothing is this more apparent than in the want of professional education and professional educators.

Pedagogy has founded universities and built its colleges and schools, and has taught many things and taught them well; but science has given to pedagogy so small a knowledge of banking that to-day it can hardly tell one whether banking is an economic institution or a branch of applied mathematics. The vast importance of a science of banking, on the one hand, and of trained educators in the subject on the other, invests every feature of the question of banking education with a twofold dignity that will command the respect and service of the best thinkers of our age.

In view of all that has been said and written on the importance of this branch of education—as to who should pursue the study of banking, and why, and how, and when, and where—a mere introductory inquiry into our present facilities for instruction, or the present scope of instruction offered, may seem very limited and easy to answer. Possibly we all have thought, until we came to look into the matter, that we knew a great deal more about the present scope of banking education than we did after we had given the subject mature consideration. Whether this observation be true as to the scope of training already offered in the schools, it will at least be borne out when we pass to the inquiry, "What should be the scope of banking education?" Ask the first two men you meet on Wall Street. The first will likely tell you that banking is, of course, the total extent and limit of banking education; the other will contend that banking education, in our day, must comprehend a knowledge of everything. Either answer alone would close the controversy before it had secured an opening. The consciousness, however, that both are right, yet right only in part, and that the wide interval between them has rights of its own, will convince you that the question of the possible scope of banking education is an open one.

The American Bankers' Association took up this question about ten years ago. Under the guidance of that organization the recently established American Institute of Bank Clerks is giving it a good degree of attention. The universities, for a number of years, have not been quite silent on the subject; and now that the movement is becoming urgent, banking literature is making a serious beginning. This urgency has become apparent through the wonderful growth of banking in connection with modern business expansion, both domestic and international, and by the restless spirit of scientific inquiry characteristic of our time. The question, therefore, is rather asked than answered; it is asked with more or less of insistency by every man inside the bank, by every educator who is not a mere classical scholar, by every student imbued with the spirit of the age, and by a very large proportion of bank depositors. This latter class comprehends three-fourths of the voters of the United States, and a no insignificant number of women.

THE ADVANTAGE OF TRAINING IN THE SCHOOLS

While the scientific literature on the subject of banking is comparatively meagre, and while at the same time there is a woful lack of trained men on the corps of instruction capable of imparting the preliminary knowledge essential to an understanding of this field, a few of our leading institutions of learning have gone into the matter seriously, and opportunities for study of this kind are constantly multiplying. Leaving this side of the problem for later consideration, we may first consider what advantage may be acquired from the schools. The measure of this advantage must depend somewhat on the prospective height of the student. If his ambition is easily satisfied, a thorough knowledge of routine up to the point of his position, and an intelligent though limited acquaintance with his surroundings, will render his services of marked value to the bank. With higher aim and a broader view, his outlook will be proportionately extended, and education will have for him another meaning. But to get to the top, wherever that top may be, it may be said, in the educational sense, that one must begin at the bottom. And it must be further remembered that the lowest round of any professional ladder is not near the ground; for the average man there must be a long approach by way of natural capacity and preliminary education. By "beginning at the bottom" is not meant, therefore, as is sometimes charged, that the young man must sweep out the office and run errands at the expense of an education, while he slowly works his way; it is meant that to know banking one must know it from its foundation principles, and a knowledge of these foundation principles may not be acquired to best advantage within a single business institution. One may begin in a particular institution and by hard work begin to climb, but before he can reach the first round of the professional ladder, much less the second round or the third, still more the last, he must have a perspective broader than the experience obtainable within that particular house. A profession is necessarily based on the combined and collected experience of the many.

The old Greeks had a saying that to become an able man in any profession three things were necessary—nature, study, and practice. Rousseau but elaborates this dictum when he says: "We are born feeble and have need of power; we are born without anything and have need of assistance; we are born stupid and have need of judgment. Whatever we have not at our birth, and which we shall need when we are grown, is given to us by education. This education comes of nature, of men, and of things. The internal development of our faculties and organs is nature's education, the use we are taught to make of this development is man's education, and the acquisition of experience by means of the objects which affect us is the education of things." And Rousseau has also shown

66

that as these three educations ought to concur to their mutual perfection, we ought duly to balance our study and practice, both of which we can control, and to adapt them or direct them according to nature, which we cannot control.

ELEMENTARY EDUCATION AVAILABLE

With due consideration, then, for individual tendencies and aptitudes, and for this natural sifting and shaking of men into their appropriate places, we approach our professional curriculum by way of such preliminary education as will be of recognized utility in the bank. The penmanship, mathematics, and book-keeping of the common school are indispensable as foundation studies. So important is the high-school in our American system of education, with its varied curriculum, including commercial studies, that the Superintendent of public schools of the City of New York, addressing the Chamber of Commerce, advises employers "to give preference for positions of trust or positions involving executive ability to graduates of high-schools or colleges"; he recommends the establishment of high-schools whose teaching shall include banking, the systems of money used in different countries, systems of exchange, explanation of the settlement of balances by export and import, commercial law, "and all other matters," he continues, "which it

67

concerns a business man in these modern days to know."

Leaving the common schools, and turning to those educational agencies which have facilities for special training, the business college, under the weeding-out process adopted by the Regents of the State of New York, will furnish preparatory studies. Its ideal curriculum, as reported to the United States Commissioner of Education, is founded upon book-keeping. With this are correlated arithmetic, elementary commercial law, penmanship, business correspondence, with typewriting and stenography, business practice, including the fictitious bank, a brief of the history and geography of commerce, a little rhetoric and some practice in public speaking, an elementary knowledge of civil government, and the foundations of economics. All this, we may say, is not far outside, and much of it is within the limits of training for bank service. But the courses must necessarily be elementary and initial; the curriculum is a brief one preparatory to more intensive study.

The Young Men's Christian Associations of North America, to the number of some seven or eight hundred, offer, under the supervision of an international examiner, a course in social economics and political science, in which banking is taught historically as follows: Banking experience in the United States, New England banks—the Suffolk system; first and second Banks of the United States; the State banking system; the Sub-Treasury system; the National banking system; the English banking system; the Canadian banking system; banking in France and Germany, and banking reform. Other courses, under international examiners, include the elements of banking arithmetic, banking accountancy, and banking law.

Another elementary schedule especially designed for this class of instruction is found in the correspondence work of the American Institute of Bank Clerks. This embodies penmanship, spelling, grammar, composition and rhetoric, business correspondence, shorthand, typewriting, commercial geography, commercial and financial history, bank arithmetic, double-entry and bank book-keeping, practical banking and finance, and commercial law. It is officially announced that the operation of the Institute does not create any obligation "which might in any manner forecast the policy of the American Bankers' Association in the matter of educational work." The bank clerks of Minneapolis, united for education, have sat together under university instruction in law and political economy; individual banks and trust companies have adopted educational methods involving a respectable degree of economic culture. The American Bankers' Association looks forward to

69

the erection of "an educational superstructure in keeping with the dignity, wisdom, and pride of the bankers of America."

So far we have just begun to approach the foot of the professional ladder. But as we look up and ask for further educational guidance we realize that we have come to a lonesome place, where few meet us, and these but new-comers and inquirers themselves. Their investigations, however, have been earnestly pursued, and their advice as to the course to take will be of the highest value. Those who have written our few modest books, or who are lecturing in our colleges on banking education, may differ somewhat here and there in detail, but on one important point they all agree with the distinguished professor who said: "If I had a son I should tell him many times a day to make himself as big a man on the inside as possible." In other words, they all are of the opinion that the boy can profitably receive higher instruction from the schools, so far as the schools are prepared to give scientific and well-digested information on the subject of banking.

WHAT IS BEING DONE IN THE WAY OF HIGHER
COMMERCIAL AND FINANCIAL TRAINING

The commercial education movement at present affecting the universities of Europe and the United

States has resulted in the establishment of special departments and colleges in which, as a specialized course, banking is taught more or less fully, and always from a high stand-point. The subject of banking has a place also in the more general economic course of our leading universities, in which a number of writers of recognized authority on banking subjects occupy important chairs. The same movement has also brought about the establishment of commercial high-schools, in which the elements of banking are correlated with the economic and mathematical studies leading to the new commercial departments of the universities. And it is upon these secondary and higher courses in commerce that a proportion of the best thought of modern educators is being expended as to the scope of banking education.

In the curriculum of the Superior School of Commerce of Paris, and in that of the School of Higher Commercial Studies at Paris, banking is divided and parcelled out to courses in general accountancy, mathematics applied to commerce, history of commerce, commercial law, and political economy. The Superior School of Commerce has been taken as the model for similar institutions outside of France, notably in the establishment of the Commercial Academy in Prague, and in the foundation, by one of its graduates, of a commerical school of three grades in Turin. The Technical Institute of

Turin has a school of banking whose instruction is organized under the two heads of administration and accounting. This instruction was awarded a gold medal at the International Exposition of Accountancy at Turin. Education for the banking profession is one of the distinct objects of the Leipsic University College of Commerce, in which the curriculum is organized upon the Paris model, except that it more clearly distinguishes between theory and practice.

The Department of Commerce of the new University of Birmingham is in charge of a former professor in the department of economics at Harvard. Here the course in banking is largely historical. After a summary view of early forms of banking in Italy, Amsterdam, and Hamburg, a more detailed historical account is given, to the middle of the nineteenth century, of the system of banking then in vogue, in which notes were the principal form of credit and the chief subject of discussion and legislation. The rise and growth of the modern system of banking is then described, in which the customer's account is the chief form of bank credit used. Going outside of English experience, the comparative method is employed; the banking development, legislation, and present practice of various countries, including England, France, Germany, Scotland, and Canada are reviewed and contrasted. Particular attention is given to banking history and experience in the United States; the first and second Banks of the United States; the more important features of banking in the separate States before 1860; the beginnings, growth, operation, and proposed modification of the National banking system; and credit institutions outside that system, such as State banks and trust companies. Thus existing legislation and practice in various countries are analyzed and compared. Along with the historical study of banking, the investments in the money markets of New York, London, Paris, and Berlin are followed during a series of months, and the various factors are considered, such as stock-exchange operations and foreign exchange payments, which bring about fluctuations in the demand for loans and the rate of discount upon them. The relations of banks to commercial crises are also analyzed, the crises of 1857 and 1893 being taken for detailed study. The Course concludes with a discussion of the movement of securities and money in the exchanges between nations, and in the settlement of international demands. After a preliminary study of the general doctrine of international trade, a close examination is made of some cases of payments on a large scale, and the adjustments of imports and exports under temporary or abnormal financial conditions are traced. Such examples as the payment of the indemnity by France to Germany after the war of 1870–71, the distribution of gold by the mining countries, and the movements of the foreign trade of the United States since 1879 are used for the illustrations of the general principles regulating exchanges and the distribution of money between nations.

The University of Pennsylvania has taken up the above-described work in three separate courses; one has for its subject the history of banking in Europe; a second course deals with the history of banking in the United States; the third course is entitled Money, Credit, and Foreign Exchange. Besides these three, the following additional courses of instruction, each covering two hours per week throughout the year, are offered to those desiring to specialize in Finance: (1) A preliminary course in private finance which discusses the various forms of Money and Credit used as Funds, the Instruments of Transfer of Credit Funds, the Financial Instruments used in obtaining Funds, and the Institutions and Agents employed in funding operations; (2) a course on the financiering of railways, including the methods of capitalization, equipment, financial management, railroad bankruptcy, receiverships, reorganization, and consolidation; (3) a course in the financing of industrial trusts and corporations; (4) a course on investment and speculation; (5) a course on the history of panics and those fluctuating phenomena of business known as periods of prosperity and depressions; (6) a course on banking law and practice. This course, intended to meet the technical and legal requirements of the banking business, is thus described: It takes up the details of the organization and operation of a bank, with special reference to its legal aspects. The study of methods of organization involves a knowledge of both State and National bank Acts and the advantages to be gained under each. The rights, duties, and liabilities of the stock subscribers and of the trustees during the formative period are considered at length. After the organization has been completed, a new set of questions arise. These are grouped around rights, duties, and liabilities of bank officers: (1) Towards each other; (2) towards the stockholders; (3) towards the depositor; (4) towards the public. The authority of bank officers, its source and extent; what an officer may and may not do; for what acts he is personally liable and for what acts the corporation is liable are practical questions which the president, the director, the cashier, the minor officer, and special agent of the bank must each answer for himself.

The Ohio State University, in a special course in money, credit, and banking, offers a comparative study of the principles and methods of banking, involving the history and theory of the subject; an account of National and State banking; the clearing-house system, and a critical analysis of proposals for reform.

The study of banking in the University of Michigan "breaks into two parts, devoted respectively to theory and history." It includes a study of the nature and social functions of the bank, of the natural laws of banking phenomena, and of systems of bank regulation. It is regarded as one of the marked advantages of this university that all its departments are available to the student of any special branch, and that mathematics, law, government, and other kindred studies may be taken in connection with those arranged under political economy and finance.

The University of Chicago offers a course in banking, including a study of principles and a comparison of modern systems. This course comprehends a study of the banking systems of the United States, England, France, Germany, Switzerland, and other countries, with special attention to the matter in which each meets the problems of currency (coin, note, and deposit), reserves, discount, and exchange. The relations of the banks to the public, their influence on speculation, their management in financial crises, special dangers, and most efficient safeguards are discussed. Relative advantages and different fields of action for National banks, State banks, deposits and trust companies, and savings banks are noted, and lectures are given on the history of banking.

The course in money and banking in the University of Wisconsin is designed "to acquaint the student with the nature and functions of money and banks, the monetary systems of the great commercial nations, the laws and methods of foreign exchange, and the history of the currency systems of the chief commercial nations." It includes a practical study of the machinery of banking, of clearing, and of domestic and foreign exchange, and discusses the relative advantages of bank currency as compared with government notes.

The department or school of mercantile and financial administration of Dartmouth College is intended to be post-graduate. "Leaving the business colleges," we are told, "to do their work for clerks, and the high-schools to teach the rudiments of accounts, and such as will to offer courses that are parallel to the regular college courses, it boldly limits itself to picked men who have completed at least three years of college work." Banking is presented under three heads—law, organization, and operation. It includes a detailed study of the bank laws of the United States and of typical States, the organization of banks for business, banking methods, clearing-houses, various forms of credit transactions, relations of banks to the public, their management in times of crisis, National, State,

77

private, and savings banks; loan and trust companies, money and exchange brokers, stock and produce exchanges and their practical working, the banking problem in the United States, and a comparative study of British and Continental banks.

A list of the studies pursued in Columbia, Cornell, Johns Hopkins, Brown, Western Reserve, Barnard, Minnesota, Radcliffe, Vanderbilt, Stanford, Yale, Princeton, and other higher institutions of learning, especially in the commercial departments of the Universities of Iowa, Vermont, and California, brings into further relief the historical, theoretical and legal aspects of banking, and emphasizes the fact that, with a strong current setting in everywhere towards the practical, the subject is approached in the United States on its economic side, as in Europe it is viewed by educators in the light of mathematics.

DEPARTMENT OF COMMERCE, ACCOUNTS, AND FINANCE OF NEW YORK UNIVERSITY

New York University has a department of commerce, accounts, and finance which, as announced by the chancellor, "differs from the several schools of finance and commerce established by prominent universities in America, in that its entire instruction is intended to be professional in character." My own relation to the Faculty enables me to state, with some fair degree of fulness, the view of the scope of banking education held by our distinguished professor of political economy and practical banking. The course of training in the principles and practice of banking, professedly " of positive and practical value to any young man who wishes to prepare himself for usefulness in the office of a bank or kindred financial institutions," is correlated with the general study of the principles of finance, the value of money, the demand for money, circumstances affecting this demand, the supply of money, metallic money, monometallism and bimetallism, investment and speculation, international balances, the mechanism of foreign exchange, payments between countries having different standards, the money market, panics and crises, the theory of credit, and a discussion of the proposed reforms of our monetary system. A presentation of banking theory leads to a historical review of the bank-note system and of banks of issue, the Bank of England, the Bank of France, the Bank of Germany, bank-note issues in the United States, our National banking system, National bank-notes, and a discussion of the " Independent Treasury" question. Banking itself, in this professional course, is viewed as an imposing financial edifice, resting on the broad foundations of political economy, alive within with the hum of all the machinery of credit, and in vital touch with every other institution of the commercial world. Its functions, of which credit is the one important element, are classed under the three heads of deposit, discount, and issue. Its dependence for profit is located at the credit centre of the community. Its credit assets are described and classified; and according to the class of these assets the bank is studied as a commercial bank, collateral loan bank, or savings bank; and these three kinds of banks, with their three several rates of interest, are treated at length. The double service performed for society by banking is noted; and the bank thus again undergoes examination as rendering credit available and as bringing capital into the hands of those who can use it to the best advantage. This brings up a discussion of wise and unwise extension of credit, of inflation, and of their effect upon prices and capital. The clearing-house and its administrative machinery are described, and the historical development of the clearing-house system is studied. The bank-note and the bank deposit are compared in their relation to the question of debt and the amount of reserve needed, and the different services performed for society by the note, on the one hand, and the deposit on the other, are carefully distinguished. The effect of legal restraint upon issue is discussed, and the various bank-note systems growing out of governmental regulation are described. Conditions of safety are stated, and security, convertibility, and elasticity in the performance of its functions by the bank-note are treated exhaustively. Branch banks and quasi-banking institutions are treated as to their relations to the general system and as to their methods of procedure. And the Course throughout, it may be added, is perhaps as fully descriptive of routine as a due regard for theoretical and historical unity will permit, or as is necessary in view of the cognate course in law and practical accountancy.

The institutions and associations at whose educational courses we have glanced—and to extend the list would hardly increase the variety—approach the matter of banking from different directions, and according to the views thus obtained their curricula take on distinctive features: Theory, practice, and the idea of being eminently and only practical; economics, applied mathematics, and Italian accounting or *ragioneria;* university convenience, the will or wish of a founder, and the pressure of public demand; academic and even political predilection on the teaching side, and on the part of the student leisure and opportunity, on the one hand, and immediate necessity, on the other; all these and many other considerations have given color, and not only color but limitation, to the various programmes of banking study. Our present inquiry, however, is not concerned with individual limitation, but with collective extent of suggestion.

When we have gathered up these suggestions, and added the few that present themselves as natural corollaries, we must confess that we have in outline a body of banking lore and instruction that ought to lower the conceit of any man who thinks he has an original conception of what constitutes a course in banking education.

THE PART OF TRAINING THAT MAY NOT BE OBTAINED IN THE SCHOOLS

Yet, in the face of this developing giant of pedagogy, which already carries a portfolio of studies—in banking law, banking theory, banking practice, banking history, banking economics, banking utilities and facilities, banking organization, banking administration, banking statistics, banking relationships, banking accountancy, banking mathematics, banking methods, and a little of everything on banking problems and questions unless it be the religion and personal appearance of the bank itself —in face of all this, a Boston economic writer says that banking is only a little money, an unmeasured amount of character, prudence, forethought, and integrity in the banker, and an unlimited amount of confidence on the part of the community. Whatever of fallacy may appear in this form of statement, the religion and the personalities of banking may not be altogether overlooked. A study of bank ethics is one of the tacitly recognized occupations of the modern business mind. This quiet study has already evolved a body of moral sentiment, of silent though powerful authority in the commercial community. And this body of thoughtful, stern, and upright sentiment, in the performance of its moral functions, looks down into the soul of every living representative of the bank, and lays a weight of accountability alike upon the boy who is saucy at the telephone and upon the board of directors which allows the bank to be robbed through some hole in a decayed system of financial accounting.

The *personnel* of banking is of primary importance as an object of educational thought, because it is with living beings that banking people have to do. Depositors, with their common rights, their liabilities, their individual cares and anxieties, and even their idiosyncrasies, will not be excluded; the shareholders will have to be measured. It is to the collective make-up of the body of workers in the bank, their official relations one with another, and their professional duties individually that the student must devote his care to know with some degree of thoroughness and familiarity. Such knowledge comes largely of practice in the path of promotion. The true scope of banking education embraces mutual official acquaintanceship among the workers, so that the clerk must know a good deal concerning the administrator's duties long before he himself takes on executive functions. Certain departments of banking knowledge are self-contained. As an illustration, take the case of the general book-keeper, whose duties call for technical knowledge known only in a general way outside of his own department. It is well known that one may advance from the lowest round of the banking ladder to the responsible position of cashier, and still be ignorant, without detriment to his own office, of the special duties and details of that of the general book-keeper. Banking culture embraces a general mutual knowledge of individual functions, such as might be compared to an *ésprit de corps;* this mutual knowledge, or collective intelligence, is an important organizing force in the inter-relations of President, Vice-President, Cashier, Assistant Cashier, chief clerk, collection clerk, country book-keeper, dealers' book-keeper, ledger-keepers, discount clerk, note teller, receiving teller, paying teller, general book-keeper, and all other employés of the bank.

If, however, the clerk for his training relies on his own experience, and on contact with his fellows in service, he must fall far short. Banking Accountancy should include, not only such advanced knowledge of the art of book-keeping as will enable one to handle the accounts of the bank intelligently, but a fair comprehension of the relations of auditing to the clerical keeping of the accounts; both banker and book - keeper should also have some conception of the value of an independent examination of the affairs of the institution as well as a proper appreciation of the administrative importance of the introduction of scientific systems and methods of accounting which are in keeping with the magnitude and variety of modern financial transactions. It is for the want of a business culture adequate to the grasp of this latter conception that uncanny losses of millions of dollars still continue to startle the half-awake consciousness of the public mind.

Banking mathematics embraces some of the most difficult and complicated calculations. Mathematics, as we have seen, is the viewpoint of banking education in the higher commercial teaching of continental Europe; and it is in this light, for its indispensable connection with the study of banking statistics, that it assumes importance as a branch of the professional study of banking.

Banking law, studied as a department of banking education, will not, indeed, make every banker and bank clerk his own lawyer; far from it, for as long as law remains a human institution it will be as complicated as human relations and cannot be mastered by the layman. A general acquaintance, however, with the principles of commercial law, and of their application to banking life, is a kind of institutional hygiene warding off the millions of unseen evils that fill the social atmosphere in which the activities of that life are conducted.

Banking history, as truly as any other department of history, is the story of a development. It is said of one banking house in London that its history from the time when it was a goldsmith's shop, with the sign of a grasshopper hanging without and only a strong-box within in which the neighbors might deposit their money, up to the present time, unfolds the whole story, chapter by chapter, of English banking. An American writer on banking says that a complete theory of banking might be constructed from events and experiences that have taken place on our continent, and that all the wisdom and all the folly of the ages as to banking have been exploited on our shores within the space of less than three hundred years. To one who would embark on this sea of life, a most instructive and thrilling tale of adventure is this story of banking development. And by its side is banking biography. The amiable Rogers, of "Pleasures of Memory" fame, was a London banker, and so was Grote, the distinguished historian of Greece, and Ricardo, the founder of the Ricardian School of Economics.

Banking, studied as a branch of scientific economics and in its relation to the science of economics, carries the curriculum into the very heart of the science of getting on in the world. Jules Simon, a French Minister of Public Instruction, once said: "Do you know what economics is? It is the science of common-sense. It first of all shows you where to look for your interests, and that is a primary service; and then it teaches you not to put them where they do not belong, and that, perhaps, is a service as great."

COMBINATION OF THE SCIENTIFIC AND THE PRACTICAL

Banking science and banking art are legitimate divisions of banking education. *Theory* and *practice* are often at variance, but it must be admitted that we are prone to extremes in this matter, either too theoretical and unpractical, or too vainly "practical" and unthinking. A story is told of the poet Southey, who was a hard worker and a very methodical man, that he once explained to a good Quaker his habit of dividing time into little parts and filling up each part with its appropriate work; one thing for this hour, another for that, and so on all day and every day and far into the night. The Quaker listened to the end, and then calmly said: "Well, but, friend Southey, when does thee think?"

These suggestions as to what constitutes the

essentials of professional education in banking have been gathered from whatever sources were available, and are modestly offered in the hope of being able somewhat to assist our educators and bankers in their effort to keep the standard abreast of the times. "Banking," says Proudhomme, "is the queen of negotiation." And one would need to be king of economic science and of business practice who would prove the master of so shrewd a mistress. But the crowning feature, they say, of our American shrewdness is that we are teachable. And as an illustration of how the American metropolis is becoming, if, indeed, it has not already become, the money centre of the world, I will repeat what a former importer of raw silk—now Mayor-elect of this city—has related of our home silk manufacture. The people of Lyons, he tells us, once thought they knew all that was worth knowing about silk manufacture, while the silk manufacturers of Crefeld and Zurich thought they knew it all. So Crefeld would not learn from Zurich and Lyons; Lyons would not learn from Crefeld and Zurich, and Zurich would not learn from Crefeld and Lyons. But the American silk manufacturers knew that they did not know all that could be known about it, so they sat at the feet of all three and learned from each one. That is the great reason why Americans have progressed so rapidly and have gone so far in so short a time; that is, they are teachable. What we want is a body of scientific knowledge as a basis for teaching and the specialized school as the basis for a profession. With these the art of banking will profit from the co-operation of a well-trained corps of bankers.

IV

THE POSSIBILITIES OF THE PROFESSION OF
ACCOUNTANCY AS A MORAL AND
EDUCATIOAL FORCE[1]

IT was with exceeding regret that I could not be
with you at your annual meeting. Had it not
been for certain engagements, and a number of
pressing invitations to attend important gatherings
in London, I would gladly have curtailed my tour
of the Mediterranean and the Dardanelles and re-
turned home by direct route from Gibraltar. It
affords me very sincere pleasure again to meet my
colleagues and companions of the New York State
Society of Certified Public Accountants.

Returning at this time, some impressions gathered from the Annual Council Dinner of the Institute of Chartered Accountants in England and
Wales, on which occasion I was your representative,
may not be out of place. At this dinner I was particularly impressed with the cordial fellow-feeling
entertained by our professional brethren of Great
Britain for the members of the recently organized

[1] Address to the New York State Society of Certified Public
Accountants, June 11, 1900.

New York State Society. Notwithstanding the fact that the war fever, just then at its very height, absorbed nearly all the enthusiasm of the meeting, your representative came in for a good English welcome. To concretely illustrate their enthusiasm, and in this I trust that you will not think further allusion vain, I quote from a published report of the meeting. President Cooper, in his introduction, referred to us in the following manner: "We are fortunate in being able to welcome to-night the President of the New York State Society, a very useful body, I believe, but a body which, I am afraid, as American affairs go, will very soon grow and exceed the whole of us." Vice-President Harmood-Banner, in proposing "The Guests" as a toast, said: "We are glad to welcome among our guests the President of the Irish Society, Mr. Jamieson of the Scottish Institute of Chartered Accountants, and Mr. Haskins, President of the New York State Society. I will ask you to remember what an honor we feel it to be to have these gentlemen among us to-night, and call upon you to drink their health, coupling with the toast the names of the Duke of Abercorn, and Mr. Manisty, the President of the Incorporated Law Society." The Duke of Abercorn, responding, said: "The President and Vice-President have referred to Mr. Haskins, who represents the United States. Possibly before many years have passed we may ask his countrymen to become the allies of this country. They are so in word at the present time; possibly hereafter they may be so in deed."

For myself, I assure you, I esteem it an enviable happiness that my lot has been cast with the worthy and honorable profession, Certified Public Accountancy, and I embrace this occasion to express to you my keen appreciation of the honor you have conferred upon me in re-electing me, in my absence, as your President for the ensuing year. I assure you that I will continue to give to the interests of the Society my careful attention, as it has been my earnest endeavor to do in the past. Referring to your appointment of me as a member of a committee to consult with the heads of certain educational institutions, looking to the establishing of a School or College of Accountancy, I am glad to be able to report very satisfactory progress. It is hoped that when we meet again in the Fall the committee which you also empowered your President to appoint, in furtherance of this matter, will be able to report to you the details of a plan agreed on.

Aside from all personal interest in Accountancy, I hold our common calling, gentlemen, in the highest honor and admiration—not only for its worthy record of achievements already past, but for the stupendous possibilities within its grasp as one of the moral and educational forces of the modern world. While abroad, I heard with sorrow of the death of a revered uncle of mine—a clergyman who had honored his title of Doctor of Divinity, who was loved and respected as the oldest rector in our American "City of Churches," and for many years was one of the three clergymen of New York collectively known as "the triumvirate" of spiritual power. With inward satisfaction, however, I read the appreciatory obituary accounts of this worthy man. And, reading thus, I was led seriously to compare the relative opportunities for good afforded by the venerable profession of Divinity and by our young profession of Accountancy. I have no sympathy with the talk that the pulpit has been superseded by the modern newspaper, or by Literature, or by Science; but neither, on the other hand, will theological teaching of itself ever impart to the pulse of business life that tone of moral health which accrues, or is earned, as it were, in the sturdy exercise of the true and intelligent accounting that belongs to commercial rectitude. In the same sense, I contend that our profession is a moral force.

Educationally, also, as well as morally, the science of Accountancy represents a power of which we are not as yet fully conscious. Its principles are so identified and interwoven with the affairs of human existence that it is as necessary for the boy with his first trousers to know and recognize just what does and does not belong in his little pocket as for the financiers of an empire to understand the state of the Treasury. Monsieur Lefèvre, Secretary to the Rothschilds, in a pamphlet published some years ago, contends that the first or elementary rules of Accountancy belong to the domain of primary education; that they are more easily apprehended than those of arithmetic, to which they should lead up as question leads to answer or inquiry to discovery; and that, with Accountancy in this extreme simplicity as a foundation, the student easily advances to that which is more and more intricate, learning, meanwhile, habits of order, of classification, of method, and of analysis, discovering thereby his own improper tendencies, and preparing himself almost unconsciously for the later study of whatever profession he may choose to embrace.

All the learned professions recognize the importance of educating the community intelligently to appreciate their labors. Physicians write our popular books of hygiene, and esteem it their greatest pleasure to give the healing potion and preventive advice to the best-informed among their patients. The legal practitioner is not covetous of a client to whom law and equity are mysteries too profound for his untutored comprehension. Theology becomes self-propagative by advancing for special education those laymen who, as learners, have already given promise of becoming worthy teachers. The best preacher is he who educates his hearers, and the best and most highly appreciated physician or lawyer is he who wisely guides his patient or client to the intelligent avoidance of disease or litigation. We, as Certified Public Accountants, have assumed this true professional attitude of public-spirited men, solicitous of the welfare of the business world at large as well as of our own immediate clientele; and our very existence as a brotherhood of such men is inspiriting among those whose good luck we seek—an educational movement, or, shall I say, an educational inquiry, that is already redounding to the social advancement of our own profession. Therefore, I say that Accountancy, in the attitude in which we have placed it, is an educational force.

And, as the rudiments of Accountancy belong to the education of all as well as of the expert, of infancy as well as of maturity, so, if we look at the matter in a historical light we find traces of a general elementary knowledge of our calling in the history of the world's childhood. We speak of our professional brotherhood as modern, and forget, sometimes, to ask whether our work itself may not be very ancient. Financial antiquities constitute a vast, unexplored region, from which, however, any adventurous spirit who plunges into its gloom for some particular purpose always returns with enough lore to pay him for his research. For example, that great classical scholar and historian of ancient civilization, Professor Mahaffy, of Trinity College, Dublin, doubting an assertion of Sir John Lubbock that banking is an institution of British origin, recently dived down into antiquity and turned up again at his *alma mater* reeking with information as to banks of all kinds everywhere, and in the very farthest corners of the ages, with all the Accountancy implied in their existence. Throughout the whole of the old Greek plays, he tells us, there are allusions to banks and bankers. The people, he says, did not keep their money at home, but gave it in charge of the banker, on whom they made out orders when the money was required. The States of Greece, says the Irish Professor, stored their treasures at great distances from home, and it is perfectly certain, he says, that the money was transferred by letters of credit or some such means. He adduces a document dealing with the repayment of a loan by the Joint Stock Bank of Athens and Delos, and mentions a case where ancient bank directors were pulled into the street and beaten because they charged too much interest. The private bank of Pasian of Athens had a capital of fifty talents, equal, according to Professor Mahaffy's computation, to £12,500, or $62,500.

A somewhat peculiar line of professional work

has interested me incidentally in the history of Accountancy as connected with governments and municipalities. In no other sphere of financial control do we find so glaring a discrepancy between the ideal and the real, and perhaps in this respect the typical meeting of extremes is seen in ancient Greece. I have in my library a large oil-painting of "Prometheus Bound," which has been said to represent very fitly the ideal side of this subject. The name of Prometheus means "forethought." He was the friend of man, to whom he gave the science of mathematics, the art of getting along, and the heavenly fire of reason. He incurred, by his fidelity, the vengeance of the awful Jupiter; and when he was hurled, with the rock to which he was bound, down to Tartarus, he flung back his defiant prophecy of a coming rectitude that should be greater than a great but unjust god. In this character of Prometheus in his "forethought," in his friendliness, in his artful getting at things, in his fire of reason, in his mathematical accuracy, in his fidelity, in his adherence to truth, it is said that the old Greeks have transmitted to us the mental ideal of a perfect Accountancy.

But while Prometheus may typify the imaginary or mythological Greek, the real Greek was another man, and Greek Accountancy was altogether another matter. As I recently walked about the streets of Athens, and looked upon the crumbling reminders of a stupendous wealth, whose corrupt administration, however, compassed the downfall of the greatest nation of antiquity, I wrote to a friend, in all sincerity: "I'm full to surfeiting of ruins." Professor Boeckh, of Berlin, whose works have almost reproduced the whole social and political condition of the ancient Athenians, tells us that they had an elaborate system of financial administration, including all the machinery necessary to a strict accounting; he draws, however, a dark picture of the morals connected with the working of that machinery. Frauds and embezzlements were of common occurrence. Nobody believed anybody. Many of the officials immediately accountable for the disposal of public funds were either slaves or citizens of very low condition; and another German writer, Professor Hudtwalcker, assures us that more credit was given to the disposition of a slave upon the rack than to the testimony of a citizen under oath. The highest administrative officers, however, made a show, it would seem, of strictness and severity in their control of accounts. Even the incorruptible Pericles, as we learn from Aristophanes, was put by them to great perplexity with regard to an item of ten talents in his account, entered as "expended for necessary purposes," but which the auditing officers readily allowed when it was explained that the sum had been employed in bribery, and that the recipients could not be named in the account without offending the Spartan King.

As we owe to the Germans our knowledge of Finance and Accountancy among the Greeks, so we are indebted to the French, especially to the publicist Gustave-Amédée Humbert, for what may be gathered of the financial economy of the Romans. And in Rome, also, the picture of administration is one of ever-increasing corruption. The best and the worst that can be said is that the very machinery of honesty and financial integrity was run in the interest of fraud and defalcation. Professor Dill, of Oxford, and now of Belfast, has shown, in a recent work on the fall of the Western Empire, that emperor after emperor endeavored in vain to stem the awful current of greed that was sweeping their nation on to extinction, and that not the Huns, not the Goths, not the Vandals, but the Romans themselves were the wreckers of Rome.

We know that Mahomet, himself the son of a merchant, and in early manhood the commercial agent of the wealthy widow whom he afterwards married, endeavored to inculcate among his followers that proper regard for the orderly keeping of accounts for which the Certified Public Accountant contends; for in the second Sura of the Koran we read: "When ye bind yourselves in debt to one another for a time, write it down. Let a writer write between you in righteousness. Let not the writer refuse to write as God hath taught him. Let him write; and let the debtor dictate, fearing God and not diminishing aught of the amount. If the debtor be weak or foolish, and not able to dictate, let his agent dictate in all honesty. And call ye two men witnesses from your neighborhood; or, if there be not two men, call to witness one man and two women, that if one woman forget the other may remind her; and let not the witnesses refuse the call. Disdain not to write down thy debt, whether large or whether small, until the day of payment; for this is right before God, right and more easy for witnessing, that ye doubt not.

"And when ye sell to one another, take ye witnesses. Hurt not the writer nor the witness; for this shall be counted for unrighteousness unto you.

"And fear ye God, O true believers; and God will teach you; for God knoweth all."

Perhaps some coming history of Pontifical finance may yet enlighten us concerning control of European treasure in the Middle Ages. Before the beginning of the Peter's-pence payment, in the early part of the tenth century, or, at the earliest, before the obligation of tithe, in the eighth, we have almost no information concerning the Pope's revenue, while outside of the Vatican there is generally supposed to have been no central national chest in Europe for ages. Professor Herbert Fisher, of New College, Oxford, writing of that later organization known as the Holy Roman Empire — of which Voltaire said that it was neither holy nor Roman nor an Empire—adduces, as a historical curiosity, an account rendered in 1242 to Conrad IV., which shows that a miscellaneous tribute, partly in kind, partly in money, had been levied by a royal bailiff in the royal borough; that Jews, farmers, litigants, and traders had paid their quotas as distinct classes of the community; that there were profits arising to Conrad on the sale of wine and on the rent of houses; and that large sums had been collected from the "enemies of the Empire," who were breaking the peace and infesting the roads. The document states that the royal bailiff is not able to add up these sums properly, because his arithmetic has been neglected; but he remembers distinctly the separate items. The expenditure is far in excess of the receipts. The bailiff has manufactured engines of war, hired cross-bowmen and knights, and made costly expeditions on the imperial service. His house has been burned, his wine has been drunk, his bread has all been eaten up, and his land has been ravaged by fire. For sixteen long weeks he has kept together, at his own expense, a force of forty men-at-arms for the Emperor, and he has as yet received nothing for it all. And, to make things worse, he has just been ordered to dismiss his captives, whose ransom might have covered the deficit. This is a fair example of the way the business of a king was transacted on the Continent at least a hundred years subsequent to the establishing of the Exchequer of England.

It would be interesting to know just when the Exchequer of England was established, and whence it came. Professor Robertson Smith, in one of his antiquarian dictionaries, takes us back to the Roman period, and says that no town, throughout the whole length and breadth of Britannia, is known to us in respect to its internal history and the details of its constitution, and that the existence of administrative machinery is a matter of inference—inference, he thinks, of the most legitimate kind, but still inference. Some of the best constitutional historians of England incline to the belief that her accounting system was brought over-sea by the Anglo-Saxons; while Continental writers, especially the German Professor Gneist, say that, of course, the English could not have had an exchequer before the coming of the Conqueror. Edward the Confessor had, it is evident, at least a treasury; for we are told that he pardoned a poor fellow who stole money out of his treasury, and that he once saw the devil dancing on the barrels of money in his treasury—and both of these incidents are illustrated in bas-relief in Westminster Abbey. Some think that William the Conqueror or Henry I. or Henry II. brought an accounting machinery full-fledged over the Channel from Normandy; while others, by an argument of their own, fetch the old Exchequer, by way of the Kingdom of Sicily, from the Saracens.

Richard Fitz Nigel, Bishop of London, and for many years Treasurer of the Kingdom under Henry II. and Richard I., and author of the earliest literary work in any way dealing with the accounting system of the English nation, believed the Exchequer to have come from Normandy, but admitted that many old men of his day referred to it as of Anglo-Saxon origin. Thomas Madox, a later historian, says: "As I have an equal veneration for our ancestors of the Saxon and of the Norman race, it had been equal to me in that respect, whether the one or the other of them had been entitled to the glory of being the first contrivers and institutors of the anciently great and noble Court of Exchequer." Bishop Stubbs, an eminent constitutional historian, thinks that on the whole "it might seem almost the safest plan to abstain from attempting a conclusion."

Americans are interested in the old Exchequer of the kings of England, because that unique institution is to us, as to the people of Great Britain, the one historical exemplar of national unity and of centralization of government; while to Anglo-American Accountancy it is at once the starting-point of continuous history and a worthy monitor of strict seriousness of business character. Its notched and broker tallies, its checkered cloth, and its piles of "counters" have been likened to the abacus and torn checks of a Chinese laundry; but any such facetious comparison ignores the awful Doomsday Book at one end of the account and the terrible duplicate record of the "Pipe Rolls" at the other.

The early history of American Governmental Accountancy rests upon the broad shoulders of giants, such as Albert Gallatin, Alexander Hamilton, the organizer of our Treasury Department, and Robert Morris, popularly known as "the financier of the American Revolution," who, before the establishment of any permanent department, had laid down the maxim for our future guidance that "genius and judgment will always leave open to experience a large field for improvement." Sir Robert Peel, with whom the maxim appears to have been an axiom, in preparing the mind of his countrymen for the appearance of a commission which in 1829 resolved to establish throughout all the governmental departments of Great Britain an entirely new system of accounts founded on that of the mercantile community, thus referred to the progress already made by the Americans: "Alluding to the simplification of the public accounts," says the official report, "I see no reason why, in this point as well as in others, we should not avail ourselves of the example of foreign nations — of

France, for instance, the public accounts of which were peculiarly clear; or of the United States of America, where the work was performed with equal plainness and facility." Such testimonies were, as they ought to have been, an encouragement to further improvement in our Governmental Accountancy, for neither Great Britain nor France nor the United States, nor any other nation, can afford to neglect, not alone a continuous scrutiny of its accounts, but a progressive revision of its very methods of accounting. And thus it was that while Baron von Hock, of the Austrian Court of Accounts, was writing, in 1857, that "no other nation possesses, in the organization of its finances, a system of accounting at once so simple in its conception and so perfect in its mechanism as that of France," the ingenious French themselves were seeking still further to simplify the working of that mechanism; and while American administrative machinery was admitted in Europe, while, indeed, certain patriotic Americans were standing in still, unprogressive awe before the stone statue of one after another of our early financiers, the living soul of those great men was advancing and animating successive leaders of administration to urge us forward in the perfecting of our accounting system.

In the more remote past, however, we find but the beginning of a systematic, scientific Accountancy. It remained for the modern spirit of scientific inquiry and modern financial demands for well-ordered and well-digested data to bring us to professional standards; and while we may well claim to have recently attained a professional standing, we still have much to accomplish. Our profession and our science are yet young. In the work of the improvement of the systems or methods of accounting of nations, as well as of municipalities and great business corporations, our profession of Certified Public Accountants will henceforth have an increasingly prominent share. Professor Newcomb, in a recent well-written article in the *North American Review*, tells an excellent story, which I will quote as illustrative of the value of independent specially educated experts in helping to carry on the work of the Government in various lines. In 1882, he tells us, Congress made an appropriation for improving the water supply of Washington by extending an aqueduct under the city. It intrusted the entire work to its officers. The latter knew that under the soil on which the city was erected there existed a layer of solid rock of sufficient hardness and consistency to serve for the walls of the proposed aqueduct. Accordingly, the conduit was hewn at a great length through the rock and carried to a reservoir several miles away.

"Nothing," says Professor Newcomb, "could be

said against the professional capacity of the engineers who conceived and executed this plan. They carried on the work with that economy and on those sound business principles which characterize the operations of our Government engineers. They knew everything that an engineer could reasonably be expected to know. Yet they did not know that the rock through which they were hewing their aqueduct, firm though it appeared on inspection, would ultimately disintegrate under the action of water. The inevitable result would be that, in a few months or a few years, the rock in which the aqueduct was cut would be reduced to a mass of sand.

"Had the Government," continues the relater, "been in the habit of consulting scientific experts, who were not professional engineers, on every question of science that might arise, this knowledge would have been gained before the aqueduct was projected. The liability of some hard and solid rocks to disintegrate is well known to geologists. The services of one of these men would have cost little, and a very little study would have brought out the fact that the rock in question was of this class. For want of this study a large sum, perhaps a million of dollars or more, has been wasted on the work, and now, after the lapse of seventeen years, it is uncertain whether the aqueduct will ever be made use of." This, I think, fairly illustrates the necessity of professional advice in matters of public administration.

When Danaë, daughter of Acrisius, King of Argos, was locked up for safe keeping in a treasury tower of brass, the great god Jupiter, to whom she cried, turned himself into a shower of gold and came down to her through the roof.   Perseus, the child of this marriage of earth and heaven, was then cast into the treasury chest, to the mercy of the waves and the winds.   But the chest outrode the storms; and Perseus, living to accomplish many a great enterprise, and to cut off the head of that enemy of progress and life, Medusa, became, so the myth says, a golden constellation in the starry heavens.

Our profession is the answer to a cry from the modern treasury; it has begun to render a good account of its career in the world of enterprise; and, let me add—lest a reference to the constellation of gold be thought too lofty—it already carries in its belt the scalp of more than one Medusa.

Now, gentlemen, I close with this encouraging reminder: that Certified Public Accountancy is solidly set upon Legislative basis; that our degree of C.P.A. is well guarded by University control; that the New York State Society represents the very highest moral aim of the commercial world; and that our profession is moving on to higher and still more solid ground.   We are in the march of modern events, and our history thus far as a society may encourage us, I think, to press on with steady courage, holding clearly in view the superior aims of our organization, neither depressed by any temporary discouragement that may come to us nor elated with the uniform success that we have so far enjoyed.

V

THE GROWING NEED FOR HIGHER ACCOUNT-
ANCY[1]

OUR subject may be viewed in various lights.
A historic view of the growing need for Accountancy might suggest looking backward upon
the advance of the science from its primitive surroundings to the present. If such were your desire, you have in this city the best opportunity in
the world for the study of the earliest known methods of financial accounting in a system far antedating the days of Abraham and coming down
without change to about the beginning of the Christian era. The Assyrian Department of the University of Pennsylvania has a large number of the
most ancient accounting records and other business
documents, inscribed on what are popularly known
as the "bricks of Babylon," discovered in the Tigris-
Euphrates Valley by Professor Hilprecht and his
co-workers. To trace the adaptations made from
time to time — to view the development of the
science through one civilization after another, to

[1] An address delivered at the annual dinner of the Pennsylvania Institute of Certified Public Accountants, Philadelphia,
April 15, 1901.

note its adjustments to commercial and industrial need—might aid us in our estimates of the present.

Quite as much profit might be derived from a forecast of the future. The well-being of the Accountancy of to-morrow is, in very large measure, dependent upon the faithfulness and magnanimity of the mere handful of accountants who comprise our young profession of to-day. Oneness of method and of professional aspirations, enlarged and exalted views of the worth and dignity of our calling, and a steady, studious, and conscientious aim to discharge well our obligations to the business world will insure to us as a brotherhood that universal and permanent recognition and appreciation upon which hang the hopes of higher Accountancy. In coming to a decision, therefore, as to how best to treat the subject assigned, it has seemed to me that a higher service might be rendered at this time by confining attention within the limits of present conditions and requirements.

Accountants are often asked what they mean by higher Accountancy. The expression is both definitive and emphatic. Accountancy is not bookkeeping; Accountancy, however, includes bookkeeping, as the whole includes its parts. We call it higher Accountancy merely to assert the superiority of a science, as yet but little understood, over the art of recording, which is merely a clerical application of the knowledge of a broad science to a narrow business problem. In the same way the advocates of university training in scientific economics have to speak of a higher Business Education, not because there are two such bodies of knowledge, but to distinguish a thorough grounding in the data of broad business experience and scientifically-arrived-at conclusions, which may be accepted as principles, from typewriting and other office routine which, Yankee fashion, we have so long dignified with the high-sounding title, Business Education.

Now, what is this Accountancy on which our profession is founded? It is the science of keeping track of wealth, of determining the financial condition of affairs, and whether, where and how, there is a diminution of wealth (a loss) or an increase in the form of profit. As a science it underlies all the art and all the expedients of expressing the details of income and outgo, and is in every way correlative with the twin sciences, Business Administration and Finance. It is not, in any sense, a part of these other Sciences, as is evident in the increasing dependence of the acutest administrators and financiers upon professional Accountancy for the diagnosis of their affairs and for consultative advice as to the prevention of leakage and the increase of volume. The work of the accountant is to audit the work of the book-keeper, to devise systems which will give to the financier or business manager a proper diagnosis of conditions at any time that he may call for it, and to install and to supervise more perfect systems of records. This is done that the business manager or financier may take the results, the statement of financial conditions, and of financial returns in operations, so shown by the accountant, as a basis for judgment. The conclusions of a *scientific* accountant are accepted by the manager and financier as the first premises for thinking about the various problems within their respective fields. But no definition of Acccountancy can ever conjure up any adequate notion of the scope of the science or present to the imagination a picture, even in outline, of the vast and expanding field of our professional operations.

To enlarge somewhat on the scope, or what, in general, is included in a knowledge of Accountancy: (Here it becomes evident that we are dealing with an experimental, progressive, and adaptive science of which we know as yet but little of the boundless possibilities.) A few years ago we were known, popularly, as expert book-keepers—expert, in particular, in a kind of detective work. True, expertism, especially in its application to the catching of somebody at something or other, was all the rage. This was natural, and so far all right, when some respectable depositary of funds had gone wrong and had taken himself off that there should be an examination of his accounts. After-the-fact examinations, as in the recent case of the First National Bank of New York, are still in favor and are not without value. As matters of ancient history, they swell the sum of human knowledge and add to the lessons of experience; but, happily, they do not express the scope of Accountancy.

Detective work and the rectification of innocent error, though vastly improved in the development of the science, are but incidents in the Accountancy of to-day; occasional flavors lend piquancy to the activities of the young bloods among us. I know a young man who stood beaming with delight for hours, surrounded with ledgers and other account books, explaining to a jury and a lot of lawyers how an absconding auditor, for whom President McKinley had made requisition on the Sultan of Morocco, had tapped the till of a great railroad for eight years. Prevention, however, is fast coming to be recognized as cheaper and better, in the long run, than the ferreting out of frauds and blunders already committed; and this recognition of the element of prevention is an important feature in any comprehensive view of the scope of Accountancy.

The integrity and general welfare of the business to which a body of accounts may relate is dependent, in very large measure, upon a keen and constant supervision of the books, individually and collectively; and it is now accepted as a require-

ment of good business policy that all inside auditing should be supplemented by frequent independent professional checking of the whole. This
"auditing of the auditor," as it is popularly called,
is entirely due to the development of Accountancy,
and is within the present recognized scope of the
science.

But all this leaves the books untouched. If
this were all, we would be compelled to witness,
even in court, to our own disgrace or neglect or
inadequacy, and to acknowledge that we had no
true scientific basis for our profession. Accountancy, in its progress, has developed a capacity for
so training and organizing the financial data of a
business that they may be readily commanded
and wheeled into line by the parties in interest.
By means of a properly installed and properly executed system of accounts, the administrator of
enterprise is able to-day to sum up the complicated inter-relationships of modern business. The
book-keeper is able to express financial facts clearly,
and the dishonest employé has a hard row to hoe.
These results are due to the development of professional Accountancy—to the simplification, meth-
odization, unification, and adaptation found to be
within the scope of this expansive science.

Still further: so thoroughly are the summaries
and classifications of financial data brought into
harmony with the underlying principles of busi-

ness success that it is known from experience that methods of business administration incompatible with scientific Accountancy are wrong methods. Accountancy, giving to the administrator a true financial picture both of business conditions and of operative results, discovers the points of friction and is able to lay its hand upon the disorder and to suggest, in part at least, a remedy. Let it be understood that this is not a trespassing upon the science of Administration or of Finance, but a peculiar function of Accountancy well known to the foremost leaders of modern business activities. The discovery of this vital connection, of this important bearing of business management and true accounting upon each other, is due to the advance of Accountancy itself and to the consequent broadening of the professional conception of its real scope. Thus, on the whole, we may say that, so far as we yet know anything of the higher Accountancy and its conditions, we find it broad enough to cover all requirements. We have no fear, therefore, that future conditions will not be met. We have no hesitancy in speaking of the basis of our profession as a progressive science, nor of its possibilities for future development to meet the demands of a fast-developing commercial and industrial need.

Concerning the field of our operations, it may be conjectured that the increasing multiplicity of great corporations, which was the immediate occasion of our professional existence, will continue to represent a demand for higher Accountancy far in excess of the supply. These vast organizations, and the humbler enterprises, on their one hand, and municipalities and State and National Departments on their other, present to the accounting profession a field of activity interminable and literally "white to the harvest." I will make bold even to call it a missionary field, and a somewhat discouraging one at that, whether we consider the general condition of accounts or the want of appreciation of the requirements of the situation.

The existing situation of business affairs on the whole, from the viewpoint of Accountancy, is unsatisfactory—perhaps inexcusably so in view of present opportunities for betterment. In some departments of business activity the methods of accounting are excellent, and in others the conditions are distinctly bad, very bad. Railroads have had sad experiences of the results of their old, slipshod accounting, and have profited by the lesson. There was a time when the civil engineer, who built the railroad and then became its president, devised all his own accounting and did all the auditing. For a while it looked as if administrative railroading would never catch up with its own development. Investors in railroad securities have also suffered for lack of well-digested and well-classified information concerning the financial standing of companies at the time that investments were made; a meaningless statement of returns to enterprise has kept investors permanently in the dark, and their investments have been made the foot-ball of mercenary and faithless employés. To-day, however, railroad accounting in the main is worthy of imitation; and, as a result both of experience and of enlarged enlightenment, railroad managers and railway investors are appreciative of the value of professional Accountancy.

A mere mention of the leading forms of modern business would recall the ghosts of many dear, departed cashiers and other gentlemen of trust who haunt the dreams of certain presidents and directors; just how dear they were, and whither departed, is the puzzle. What is no puzzle is that a timely adoption of properly organized accounting would have prevented the rascalities of these late-lamented fiduciaries. It might not be surprising that a big, bulky giant of a thing like a freight and passenger railroad should have its pockets picked in the crowd; that it does all its work so safely only shows that it is not as clumsy as it looks. But that such a delicate, sensitive organism as a purely financial institution can be robbed from within itself, that its own machinery is made to grind a private grist, would seem to indicate that somebody, somewhere, is not fully awake to present counting-house requirements and opportunities.

It is not easy, looking over a great nation bristling with every conceivable enterprise, to pass judgment as to which of them presents the best examples of methods of doing business and which the worst; but, looking at the matter as an accountant, and allowing for the few worthy exceptions that do not prove the contrary, I think that not far, at least, from the bottom of the list will be found the American municipality. It cannot be said in excuse of the unsatisfactory condition of our municipal accounts that a municipality is not strictly a business organization, for the municipality does business, and does it on a large scale, and does it with trust funds—and does it badly. Nor does the fault lie with individuals; it is to be found in the general want of compulsory accountability in the handling of municipal revenues.

Chicago, for example, one of the great centres of business enterprise of the modern world, has long outgrown the heterogeneous jumble of taxing bodies and the old-fashioned, incongruous methods of financial administration on which its public welfare depends. Yet there it is, with antiquated ways of accounting lingering on from year to year and presenting showings incomplete, contradictory and unreliable. No general audit is provided for; taxes have long been written off, and franchise payments have been received and vouchers paid, without any proper verification of the accounts. The departmental accounts do not form with one another a harmonious whole, so that in one statement a total valuation, a balance, or a general debit or credit will appear at one figure, and in another statement the same item or summary of account will appear at a different figure. Forced balances, omissions, arbitrary entries, even credit given for money to be received some months later, are not uncommon in the books of this great city. On the whole, the people are ignorant of the true condition of their finances; first one official, then another, is suspected of wrongdoing, merely because the books do not show whether he is all right or wrong. Chicago, within whose territorial limits examples of the best accounting systems in the world are to be found, hangs its head at the very mention of Municipal Finance. I have mentioned only one city, merely to indicate in the most general way the existing condition of municipal accounts almost everywhere. As this condition, however, emphasizes the growing need of the higher Accountancy, and as municipalities will certainly be numbered hereafter in fast-increasing proportion among our clientele, it will be seen that our profession, as well as patriotism and public spirit, furnishes a strong incentive to the study of local Finance and Government. As a rule, our city, country, and town officials are honestly desirous of acquitting themselves well, especially in their administration of the revenues, and we cannot too insistently urge upon their attention the vital connection between good administration and orderly accounting.

This matter of municipal accounting is drawing to itself of late a good share of public attention. Political on the one hand and economic on the other, with a strong flavor of morality, the whole question is commanding the consideration of eminent thinkers. Societies have been formed whose object is the betterment of local administration. One of these organizations, having its headquarters in Philadelphia, reports one hundred and nineteen affiliated Associations in the United States. Conferences have been held in several cities, a plan of city organization has been drawn up, and a complete system of municipal accounting has been outlined. The matter has been introduced into the State legislatures, and some of these have enacted laws requiring a uniform rendering of accounts. All this opens a door of opportunity for some municipality to establish a system of accounts that others will imitate.

In all that I have said, briefly and by way of outline, there must have been seen a growing need of the higher Accountancy, in the steady development of business principles, the increase of volume, the change of conditions, the growth of new enterprises, and the general ignorance of the nature and value of scientific accounting. This want has been to some extent met, as enlightenment has created an intelligent demand on the part of the public and an intelligent supply on the part of the profession. But the need will continue, the demand will increase, and the regulation of the supply will still be a problem in the hands of the profession.

This regulation demands a close and constant consideration of quality as well as quantity. Nothing is so important to the acceptability of Accountancy as to be able to give a good account of itself. Men of caliber, of aptitude, of ability, and, upon occasion, of special expert experience, are rightly demanded of us by those whose records are to be scrutinized or whose methods are to be reformed or replaced with comprehensive systems of accounts explained in detail and adapted to the broad requirements of modern affairs.

Two movements looking to this end have already made fair headway. Both of these movements are in the interests of the business world, and command the support of thoughtful men of affairs and of others in every walk of life who are at all solicitous of the economic welfare of our country. I do not mean that this support is enthusiastic; far from it. But the moral sympathy we have is sincere, it is abiding, and it is increasing. And with this general good - will of the business world professional Accountancy will work out its own destiny.

One of these movements has been for legislation recognizing and safeguarding the profession. Such legislation has no thought of acts of exclusion, but was intended to find out, and set apart, and officially recommend such as could prove themselves qualified to practise professional Accountancy. The Public Accountants Act of New York granted the exclusive right, not to practise as accountants, but to practise under the designation Certified Public Accountant, with the use of the initials C.P.A. to those who should pass an examination before a committee appointed by the Board of Regents of the University of the State of New York. Pennsylvania, Maryland, and California followed, mainly in the same line; we now have in four States a legally recognized profession of Public Accountancy.

One of the first and most important effects of this legislation has been to arouse an interest in the study of the higher Accountancy. If the motive of the student or of the applicant for a certificate were only to pass the examination much would be gained. Two facts, however, now come to light: one, that the educational aspirations of our young men were founded upon a real love for the profession; the other, that no existing educational institution even pretended to meet all these new requirements and aspirations. To legislation, then, is indirectly due the existence of the only university College of Accountancy in the world. Let us hope that the curricula of many of our colleges and universities will expand to meet the growing demand.

This suggests the other agitation to which I refer—the educational movement. Notwithstanding repeated effort, this agitation met with little success until backed, as we have seen, by the Legislature and the Regents of the State University. With official support thus obtained, application was made to New York University for the establishment of a special department of accounts, the intention being to complete the chain as follows: Recognition by the Legislature; certification by the State University, an administrative body; and preparation by New York University, an educational body. The council and chancellor of New York University, however, decided on an enlarged plan along the lines of the movement for higher commercial education; this plan included, as a special and prominent feature, a fully equipped College of Accountancy. This, in brief, is the history, which I am almost daily asked to give, of the New York University School of Commerce, Accounts, and Finance.

And thus, gentlemen, I have given you, with such illustrations as were most readily available, a few thoughts on a topic worthy of more extended consideration. I sincerely hope that what I have said may be what the old authors used to call "aids to reflection." I thank you very heartily for your patient attention.

VI

THE PLACE OF THE SCIENCE OF ACCOUNTS IN COLLEGIATE COMMERCIAL EDUCATION[1]

I AM asked to address you on "The Place of the Science of Accounts in Collegiate Commercial Education." A most hopeful phase of the subject assigned is that it recognizes a place for *higher Accountancy* in higher commercial education, and that it indicates the usual reformatory "stage of inquiry" as to what or where that place is. A discouraging feature is found in the expectation that it can be adequately treated in a brief paper. The title is worthy to head an exhaustive educational essay.

Inquiry is to-day the attitude of all economic thought. Acceptable leaders of affairs are they who "listen to the voices" and are not too characteristically dogmatic. Silent brain-forces, urged on by the shifting of conditions, are spreading their tents far over the borders of traditional authority. The right ordering of the march of modern material civ-

[1] A paper read at the Thirteenth Annual Meeting of the American Economic Association, Ann Arbor, Michigan, December 28, 1900.

ilization, with its bewildering inter-relations of interests, is a living, breathing question, involving, day by day, a million-fold entanglement of ever-new inquiries. With the unravelling of these questions, extending from the adjustment of international commerce down to the problem of auditing an auditor, our modern scientific economics has set itself, I believe, modestly and patiently to deal.

Scientific economics, in this listening and learning attitude, in scanning the horizon of the general welfare, has found a brother-spirit in the teaching science—a brother-spirit at once conservative and cautiously progressive, a science notably in love with the past but essentially solicitous of the future. And this coming together of the economic and pedagogical sciences is now taking the shape of a compact that what the one shall accumulate by way of well-digested and well-classified information the other shall disseminate. These are the active agents as well as the compacting, undeveloped instruments to be employed in the present movement for the higher commercial education. In these may also be found the present limitations to the movement.

This important subject of advanced commercial education, familiar to the nations of continental Europe, is least of all understood by our friends the English; to the English, on the other hand, we owe the introduction into the United States of the profession of Public Accountancy. According to a recent review article by the Hon. James Bryce, the phrase, "a commercial education," meant, in the England of but a few years ago, something "cheap and nasty"; and that it now means anything more respectable is due, he says, "not to reflection on the part of Englishmen, but almost entirely to the example of foreign countries, and, in particular, of Germany, France, and Belgium." Had Mr. Bryce been writing on specific education in accounting, he would doubtless have particularized also Italy; possibly he also would have included the Netherlands; he would, I think, have written France, with its bureaucratic *comptabilité*, before Germany. To the three countries first enumerated we also, in the United States, owe much of our interest in general commercial education. On the other hand, we are but little indebted to them for our knowledge of professional Accountancy.

The question as to the place of Accountancy in collegiate commercial education has not been answered in Great Britain, where, notwithstanding a sturdy Scottish and English professional Accountancy, there was no general and comprehensive system of commercial education; it has not been answered on the Continent, where, notwithstanding systems of commercial education, otherwise admirable, government book - keeping has been too often the typical Accountancy. If we are to have this question answered, we must answer it ourselves; it must be answered here in America, where conditions are evolving a profession of Accountancy side by side with professions of Finance and Business Administration.

I have often wondered what some Chaldæan school-boy of the days of Abraham would have thought of such a condition of things. We are told by the young science of Assyriology that Babylonian education, at least seven thousand years ago, was very largely commercial. Professor Sayce, of Oxford, thinks that this education began at about the age of five years; Professor Jastrow, of the University of Pennsylvania, says that whether preparatory to a governmental, religious, literary, or business career, it was commercial in character from beginning to end. Assyrio-Chaldæan educacation included a complete knowledge of the vast commerce of this commercial people, an art of accounting as advanced as their clay tablets would admit of; they had a thorough knowledge of business law. Our belief in the progress of mankind is staggered as we listen to the faint words, "commerce, accounts, and law," that fall through long milleniums upon this modern economic and educational questioning of ours. An outline of Chaldæan commercial law which I have in manuscript would almost seem to have been made from the precedents of our own times. Under "promissory notes," we read of abstract notes; of titled notes; of interest-bearing notes, divided into those providing for the payment of the interest and those "containing debts remaining unpaid"; then of notes coupled with collateral contract, such as guaranty and mortgage—a mortgage, we are told, being always a first mortgage, and becoming "void upon payment of the debt." Business combinations are divided into partnerships and joint stock companies; and we are told how they were formed, how they appointed their agents, into what classes agents were divided, and their legal powers and liability to third parties. The leasing of farmlands, of water-lots, of houses, of all rural and urban properties was fully regulated, and all manner of payments, in money and in kind, in full, in part, in advance, with amount, date, and place carefully specified, were provided for. And all these, and the rest of a complete system of commercial law, were fully understood in the Accountancy of those distant days.

We are attempting to answer this modern question as to "the place of Accountancy in collegiate and commercial education" in New York University. Our first thought was of a professional college of Accountancy alone, which should cover all branches of the science and related studies under university supervision and control. Then, as we became acquainted with this movement for the more general higher commercial education, and with the insistency of professional administration in the same direction, the Council decided to add Commerce and Finance to our proposed curriculum. In selecting a name for the new department an alphabetical collocation was suggested of the words "accounts, commerce, finance," as giving a kind of ascending importance to the title of our new college. Finally, when the pivotal place of scientific Accountancy was fully recognized, the euphonic arrangement, indicative also of the place of the science of accounts in collegiate commercial education was chosen, which has given title to our School of Commerce, Accounts, and Finance.

This pivotal aspect of Accountancy calls for serious consideration in the elaboration of curricula for collegiate, post-graduate, and professional institutions of commercial education. Accountancy, indeed, is the viewpoint of economic administration—the "conning-tower" of the ship in the battle of business. In the plotting of the field, in the study of financial principles and methods of operation, the leaders of any business enterprise, however small or great, and whether individual or co-operative, private or semi-public, municipal or governmental, ought always to be within ready reach of their accounts, and to be able at any instant to "reference back" to this central starting-point. Accountancy, in its turn, as the vital gauge and monitor located at the very soul-centre of affairs, must be able to answer intelligently and instantly any question advanced from any direction with regard to the past, present, or probable future financial condition of an enterprise or of two or more related enterprises. And the greater in magnitude the enterprise and the volume of its business, the more complicated the relations, and hence the further removed from the grasp of the administrator in person, the more imperative is the necessity for detailed scrutiny and scientific control of financial accounts. Thus has arisen among us an Accountancy in the secondary or higher educational sense, extending into an Accountancy in the deeper scientific or post-graduate sense, and further into a recognized Public Accountancy in the strictly professional sense. Here, gentlemen, are aspects of an important and importunate line of study readily adjustable to every existing university system of commercial or economic education.

If by the "place" of the Science of Accounts in this education we understand its position in the curriculum, as well as its importance as a study, I would refer again to its easy adjustability. In this relation I would add one word as to the facility with which the embryotic Accountancy already found in our commercial courses may be expanded to its just proportions. This science seeks not so insistently a change of place in any educational system as a due amplitude for the place already granted. Accountancy is a science, upon which is founded a recognizable profession—Public Accountancy—on a plane with that of Medicine, Theology, or the Law. It follows then, that keeping always in view the end or issue of any course of economic study, an enlargement and rounding out of the "accounting" now seen in European and American educational programmes will be at least a good continuation of a respectable beginning. For the present, therefore, I would advocate, as my modest contribution to this day's consultations, not any radical change of place or relationship in this important study, but a broadening of conception of such character and magnitude as will bring within the sweep of the Course, and within reach of our prospective professional public accountants and our future administrators and their assistants, a comprehensive knowledge, according to the various requirements of future individual calling, (1) of the theory of accounts, (2) of practical accounting, (3) of the historical development of Accountancy, (4) of the higher auditing and intelligent investigation, revision, and origination of methods of accounting, and (5) of the relations of Accountancy with commercial law and with municipal and general government.

I am somewhat loath, as a professional public accountant, and, therefore, a plain man of business, to offer advice which may seem to trench too closely on the peculiar province of the professional teacher, or to attempt the formulation of definitions that our lexicographers will yet gather, better made, from the future writings of learned economists. I have been so often asked, however, to state what we mean by such expressions as "higher Accountancy," and what, with some degree of particularity, should be included in the study of this science, that, in closing, I shall presume to venture one or two answering remarks.

Accountancy is not book-keeping; the use of the qualifying terms "higher," "scientific," and the like, besides rendering our nomenclature less monotonous, enables us to emphasize this important distinction. " Un excellent teneur de livres," says the eminent author of *Manuel des Affaires*, "peut être un fort mauvais comptable." The routine writing up of account books is an adjunct of financial and commercial activity with which the educated accountant must be thoroughly acquainted in its minutest details, as the physician in charge must be cognizant of the doings of his laboratory assistant or a consulting lawyer must know the details of dockets and office records kept by his clerks; but the phrase "an expert book-keeper" is wholly misleading as to the aspirations of the informed and intelligent student of Accountancy. He who understands the principles of this progressive, adaptable science would be able, under adverse circumstances, as the Chaldæans did, to pick up a lump of clay and express thereon a recording system of his own. He must know the underlying principles of diagnosis; he must know financial health as well as financial disease; he must be able not only to recognize business condition, but to prescribe remedies to restore the patient to health, and to devise systems and methods by which his client's affairs may be kept in wholesome, vigorous, working activity; he must do more— he must be able to install such a system and such methods, and train the staff of the concern for which it is devised to co-operate in reaching results in profits which will insure business success. Let book-keeping itself be studied in the light of Accountancy, and you have, wherever the caliber of the student is equal to the condition, an originator of methods and modifications of methods of keeping track of accounts and complications of accounts, and of diagnosing diseases of business and prognosticating the course of financial conditions. Accountancy, upon occasion, enters an establishment and calls, first of all, it may be, not for books, but for some little dusty bundle of vouchers, or, perhaps, an out-of-the-way fact recorded in some corner of a private safe, wholly outside the domain of the book-keeper's knowledge. And thus, if necessary, it goes through the details of the entire enterprise, accumulating a knowledge of the vital conditions of income and outgo. Once the entire truth is known, Accountancy is planted thereon as a rock, an impregnable fortress, and stands as a mathematical demonstration as unassailable as fate —an oracle to be consulted with sincerity and respect.

As to a definite course of instruction in Accountancy, I shall only suggest that this study be closely correlated with courses in Commerce and Finance, and especially with Commercial Law and Business Administration; however crudely elementary its beginning, it includes in its progress, or, better, perhaps, from its first general conception, a philosophical grasp of the theory of accounts, of practical accounting, and of auditing. More specifically, the course ought to comprehend the principles and purpose of accounts; an examination of the various modern systems and books of accounts; a detailed description and illustration of the accounts of individuals; of partners; of commercial, financial, manufacturing, transportation, and other corporations; of municipal accounts; of federal accounts; the study of receivership, trusteeship, executorship, liquidation; the making out of statements of affairs; the verification of balance-sheets and statements of profit and loss; and the rendering of general and special reports. To these studies New York University adds lectures in the history of Accountancy; and also, on account of the favorable location of our School in the heart of a great city, as well as to accommodate certain legal requirements attaching to the profession of Certified Public Accountancy, we have recommended to our students a coincident experimental study in the office of a scientific accountant. Our method of study is, for the present, founded upon the lecture system; I trust, however, the day is not far distant when the interest of pedagogical authorship will result in giving us a worthy series of text-books in Accountancy adapted to use in the United States.

VII

HISTORY OF ACCOUNTANCY

INTRODUCTORY[1]

IN this introductory lecture on the History of
Accountancy I purpose to indicate briefly and
in a general way the path we may hope to follow
in investigations into the origin and growth of the
art of "accounting," of the development of the
science of "Accountancy," and of the rise and progress of the profession of "public accountant." I use
the modest word "hope" as to following a path,
because, in the present literary and educational
condition of our subject, we are not sure of con-
secutive connections and of a continuous line of
historical information.

Everything about us is new; the novelty of our
situation is striking, from whatever point of view
we see it. Professional Accountancy, as pictured
to our self-respect and as understood and recog-

[1] Delivered at the opening of the School of Commerce, Ac-
counts, and Finance, of New York University, October 2, 1900.
Reprinted from the publications of the American Academy of
Political and Social Science, Philadelphia.

nized with ever-expanding appreciation in the world of Commerce and Finance, is as a revelation of yesterday. Professional interest in the higher education demanded of us in the spirit of a learned brotherhood, acting at the nerve-centre of a system of economics, is as yet but a fresh awakening. New York University is the first great administrative body of learning to throw wide the gates of Academe and give the young profession an educational home. The literature of Accountancy is in its infancy, awaiting, we may say, the fostering care of cultured authorship. Even the very word Accountancy, though not quite so new as the great Dictionary of the English Etymological Society would make it, is of recent coinage, and of much more recent adaptation to its present accepted use.

You will be prepared, therefore, to know that there is no printed history of Accountancy, and that, aside from one or two works of a somewhat historical bearing on particular methods of accounting, the material for such a history is not easily accessible.

If, then, we would know the story of our calling as a brotherhood, and of the scientific and artistic development of which our profession is the expression, we must do as investigators have always done: gather our facts as we can, and classify them as our knowledge of their relations may warrant. Nor should we be discouraged. In this way Sociology, though written on by the ancients, less than twenty years ago was styled by an eminent Austrian professor as "the first lispings of a great science of the future." This has already achieved a highly respectable literature. Dentistry, though it can point back to gold fillings in the teeth of Egyptian mummies, is one of the youngest of the learned professions. This young profession is based on an extensive scientific literature. And though veterinary history already tells of the discovery of a veterinary papyrus of high antiquity, still only recently it took its place to aid a science and to enlighten a profession.

Some months ago I began to collect information on the History of Accountancy, and what I have gathered I shall endeavor to lay before you. In this, however, as in all our study, we must be co-workers; and if at any time any reader of any book shall find any line of fact that may be woven into our history, I trust I may have the benefit of his acquisition.

If one were asked why it is that men seem to shrink from forgetting, why we are so curious about the doings of our grandfathers, why we delight ourselves in that which connects us with the past, answer might be made that continuity appeals to our sense of moral beauty, that while the deformity of the brusque and unaccountable offends, we are willingly drawn to the logical, the consistent, and the appropriate. But aside from any æsthetic consideration, Accountancy, as a progressive science, must be the same yesterday, to-day, and to-morrow, except that as a development it is older and wiser as time goes on. Its past, present, and future will always have the family likeness, and will pass before us hand-in-hand. To know our past, then, is the better to understand our present and to forecast or control our future. "Study your past," Confucius tells us in his *Analects*, "and you shall know your future." The educator, Froebel, says: "It is the duty of every generation to gather up its inheritance from the past, and thus to serve the present and prepare better things for the future."

But how shall we go about this search into the labyrinth of former times? Where shall we find these severed fibres that may be twisted into the warp and woof which in turn may be woven into the fabric—the history of Accountancy? Accountancy, we know, is involved in the history of nations —in the more general history of civilization, in that of commerce, of banking, of education, of mathematics, of language, and a hundred others, so that in the study of these general and special histories we may hope to find, here and there, notices more or less extended of private and governmental accounts and methods of accounting. Biography is another source of history; folk-lore, poetry, the drama, tales, and the like are a species of literature in which many a gem of our past lies hidden. For guidance, where no definite mention is made in the histories of the past, we may often assume Accountancy from circumstances, holding our opinion in solution, however, until the inference shall have been verified. Thus, as the astronomer, from signs otherwise unaccountable, assumes in a tentative way the existence of an intramercurial planet and describes and even names it, so we, from the vast commerce of nations, or from the stupendous wealth of individuals, of whose methods we at first know little or nothing, may legitimately infer their Accountancy, and attempt a modest beginning of the reconstruction of its history. But for sources of information, in large measure, the history of Accountancy must look to those records which have been overlooked or discarded by the historians whose interest has been social, political, or literary.

The general trend of our inquiry, geographical as well as chronological, will be according to the methods of accepted history, but our attitude towards authority ought always, it seems to me, to be one of a somewhat independent conservatism. We must be free, for example, notwithstanding the penchant of historians for locating all the oldest things in the world in the Nile valley, to find that, according to recent research, this cannot be done in the matter of business records. We must avoid the temptation, again, of stating for fact what is only inference in regard to the business methods of the Phœnicians. Nor may we too arbitrarily set the old Exchequer of England down as merely mediæval on account of its early date, or as modern on account of its permanent influence and its prominence in constitutional history. The reason for this independence of conclusion will be found in the fact that those who have had other interests have not as carefully sifted the data of business as we might hope to do.

PRIMITIVE METHODS

A cursory view of existing races of men will show us tribes in which no appreciable accounting, and very little counting of any kind, need be sought even to the present day. Francis Galton, during his scientific travels in Africa, found men from whom he was obliged to buy his mutton singly, or one sheep at a time, because they could not understand that for two sheep, at two plugs of tobacco each, he must give them a lump sum of four plugs of tobacco.

Outside of the traditional and well-authenticated westward flow of history, among peoples whose antiquity has not as yet been connected with this continuous stream by investigators, we find interesting accounting methods or devices which we shall be at a loss to bring together into one view, except in some arbitrary way, as a matter of mere convenience. Setting out eastward from south-central Asia, we may embark from old Cathay and cross the Pacific, using for our guiding star the immense primitive architectural structures of the Ladrones and Carolinas and the giant statuary of Easter Island, thus following a former notion, founded on the marvellous sailing abilities of the early inhabitants of the Ladrones, that America was peopled from Asia by way of the islands of the sea; or, since we have no chronology to please or offend, we may sail from Mexico or Peru, following the silver and gold of a Spanish galleon.

How did the Montezumas and the Atahualpas keep track of treasure which upon dire occasion could fill a room with gold? We are told that a device known to the Aztecs as the quipu was used for accounts; this device consisted of a twisted cord made up of strands of different colors, and from which hung a fringe of knotted strings. The knots on these dependent strings were representative of numbers, and might be so combined as to express any required amount, while the colored strands of the main cord stood, by ingenious combination, for sensible objects and even abstract ideas. The quipu was used for writing, for reckoning, and for recording, and in the latter case was deposited among the archives in charge of the keeper of the royal revenue.

In the Orient the reckoning-frame known as the Japanese soroban, the Chinese suanpan, and the Corean supan, for untold ages an adjunct of the shops of Eastern Asia, consists of a series of stretched wires or threads, on each of which a number of balls or beads are strung. On this calculating contrivance the sedate Chinese merchant, the polite little Japanese shopwoman, or the Corean school-boy " plays with the fingers," says a recent writer, " as on a musical instrument, grasping whole numerical cords." This useful accompaniment of Asiatic mercantile life, sometimes appearing as an elegant and expensive little pocket piece, is essentially the same as the Russian tschotu, which has found its way, through France, into our Kindergarten and other schools. Along with the suanpan, our Chinese laundrymen have made Americans familiar with their mutual-safety record of deposits as represented by the torn check; this, in principle, is identical with the split tally of Europe; and it is evident, whatever their origin, that methods of accounting approximating our own are not new to the Mongolians. The author of *Village Life in China* tells of a common retail butcher who kept fourteen different account books, and the autobiographical writer of *A Japanese Boy* says that before the influx of Western civilization his people could solve algebraic problems, and that his copy-book at school was made from leaves of an old ledger which recorded the debits and credits of his grandfather.

Across Asia, to the west, in what we call the Orient, and of earlier origin than the counting-frame, with its wires and balls, was the dusted or sanded board for holding pebbles, or counters, laid along lines or grooves drawn with the fingers. This was the Oriental abak, afterwards known as the Greek abaks and the Latin abacus, the word abak meaning dust or sand. At first the stones were laid in grooves drawn with a stick in the sand at the calculator's feet. To this day, in the out-door schools of the Brahmans, the first arithmetical exercises of the children are in the sand. If we may suppose the quipu, which could be filed away as a record, to have been some dis-tant development out of the suanpan, a mere cal-culating machine, and this to have been derived from the early Oriental notion of the abacus, we shall have a geographical indication of the cradle of civilization not at variance with accepted his-tory as corroborated by all recent research.

EARLY RECORDS

The earliest regular commercial and financial records of whose chronology we have any certain knowledge are found in what are historically called the first group of nations—that is, in the countries south and east of the Mediterranean, especially in the Nile and Tigris - Euphrates valleys. The archive chambers and counting-houses of Babylon and Assyria have recently given to the spade of the excavator hundreds of thousands of business books and documents, collectively known as "contract tablets," of such astoundingly ancient dates that the mind almost refuses to believe the signed and sealed writings. These enduring witnesses to the vast antiquity of commerce, accounts, and finance, inscribed in cuneiform or wedge-shaped letters on little slabs and cylinders of baked clay, have been standing for thousands of years upon the shelves of business and government offices and libraries, awaiting the call of the modern archæologist to come forth and to describe to us the methods of business procedure of those distant ages; these same bricks bearing their Eastern language are found far west in Upper Egypt. The caravans of Eastern commerce were mail-carriers; in the West were schools in which the bewildering syllabary of Babylon and the Semitic and Sumerian tongues were taught; and the centre of this literary activity, we are told by the Orientalist, was Canaan.

The Jews in Canaan, devoted rather to agriculture and the pastoral life than to commerce, have, nevertheless, left us, in their sacred writings, instructive and beautiful pictures of the spirit of Accountancy, especially as controlling the relations of man to his Maker. And it may be said of that nation that, as the storms of the ages have uprooted their successive homes and driven them into the compact ways of brainy financiers, they still retain, in worthy measure, the sturdy business integrity of the old exile of Chaldæa.

Egypt, the land of the papyrus, was a country of scribes. Everything was recorded, even to monumental descriptions of the recorders themselves. These men, more or less, according to position or capacity, did all the book-keeping, all the auditing, all the rendering of accounts. Their book was a papyrus roll; their pen was a reed from the banks of the Nile; their inks were red and black, and their ink-stands were little pots fitted into a wooden hand-palette. In the chiselled and painted pictures of the glory of the Pharaohs we find these accountants keeping track of all the items of the vast royal revenue, of the income and outgo of every slave's back-load of wheat in the granaries; and if anything is missing anywhere, we are sure to have somewhere a description of the hunt for the shortage and the fixing of responsibility under the guidance of the gods of light.

Tyre and Sidon were centres of a world - commerce controlled by the Phœnicians, or, as some think, by the Arabians in the more general ethno-

logical sense. This commerce, which wafted the
ships of the sea far out beyond the Pillars of Hercu-
les, and guided that "ship of the desert," the camel, in his northern, eastern, and southern voyages,
traded everywhere in Tyrian purple, in Oriental
pearls and gold, in the spices of Arabia, in African
ivory, panthers' and lions' skins, and slaves; in
Egyptian linen, in Grecian fine wares and pottery,
in Cypriote copper, in Spanish silver, in Elba's iron,
in English tin, and in the amber of northern Germany. We know nothing of the Accountancy of
this great commercial nation, but in this connection
a suggested solution of another question is incidentally very interesting. How did the Phœnicians,
who are not known to have been a literary people,
come to invent the alphabet? Merely for purposes
of book-keeping has been one of the suggested answers. Trading on the Egyptian coast, it was tan-
talizing to them, we are told, to behold the educated accounting officers, in a priestly picture and
word-sign writing which it would take half a life-
time to learn, keeping a perfectly intelligible account of all the loadings and unloadings of the
foreign vessels. And so, setting themselves to in-
quiring and inventing, they at last evolved, out
of the few accidental simplicities contained in the
lumbering old Egyptian vehicle of thought, a little alphabet of sound signs that might be so combined into words of their own as to express their

debits and credits and keep them from being cheated. And this, it is thought, would account for the Greeks having remembered them as inventors of the alphabet.

The classical languages abound in words and phrases belonging to an early Accountancy more elaborate, however, than that of the Egyptians. Greek and Roman writers, but especially the later legal minds, have left us, all in all, a fair picture of what they thought Accountancy, in its inner spirit, ought to be. Many documents, some of them— as, for example, the recently recovered waxed tablets of Pompeii—of a highly interesting character, have thrown much light on the business methods of the Latins and the earlier Greeks. A few German and French writers have laboriously reconstructed this department of classical life; and one work, at least, minutely describing the governmental Accountancy of the Athenians, has been translated into English. Coming to the study of this subject predisposed, as we all are, in favor of many Greek and Roman ideals, we soon learn not to look for too much from Greek and Roman reality; and as we trace the causes of the sapping of life to the final fall of these greatest nations of antiquity, and apply our reflections to our professional calling, we see that defective Accountancy may become the hand-maid of financial corruption.

The light of historical investigation is slowly dispelling the gloom of the Middle Ages, but as yet, aside from the Exchequer system, we know little of methods of accounting from the downfall of the Western Empire to the Reformation. Mohammed was a business man, and gave his followers, in his moral writings, the benefit of much of his practical knowledge and wisdom; in the Koran we find creditable directions for the conduct of commercial life, including, in the second chapter, explicit instructions in regard to the recording of sales and loans. A knowledge of pontifical finance would, doubtless, reveal a settled method of keeping track of the revenues of the Church; but we are told that in northern Europe royalty had no central chest up to a very late period. We may suppose that the mercantile class were, as a rule, very deficient in even elementary knowledge of counting-house affairs before the establishment of secular and burgher schools.

A number of side-lights have been thrown on the Accountancy of the Middle Ages by controversy as to the origin of the Exchequer. Those who would bring the system, even in embryo, from the continent with the early Saxons, have little proof of methods of accounting existing where the folk-land, or public domain, as constitutional historians tell us, "was the standing treasury of the country." But that the kings of England before the time of the Conqueror had a centralized system of finance

151

and a treasury, with its officers of receipt and disbursement, is generally admitted except by certain continental writers. Even here, however, the clew is lost far this side of the Britain of Roman days. The contention for a Norman origin has in its favor the similarity of the systems on both sides of the Channel and the fact that the early financiers of the Exchequer and of the royal household had come from the French side. Aside from the advocates of all these views, others have attempted a more or less remote connection of the Exchequer of England with the Saracens.

Perhaps there has nowhere appeared in history a more picturesquely interesting show of profitable royalty than this boisterous Exchequer of merry old England. Beside a great table covered with green cloth, which had been marked with chalklines, somewhat after the manner of an ancient counting-board, sat the gowned and bewigged dignitaries of the kingdom; and before them waited criers, ushers, calculators, and other officers, and, perhaps, a number of tax-payers with grievances against the sheriff of some provincial county, who was about to appear with his quantum of revenue in cash and in kind collected in accordance with the quota demanded by the great census and inventory record known as Doomsday Book. In a court contiguous to the Exchequer building the sheriff has left hawks, horses, and other articles accepted as taxes for the King, and has received therefor, according to valuation, receipts in the shape of tallies. The tally is a little stick of dried wood, with crosswise notches cut by the receiving officer to represent the amount credited; this was split lengthwise across these notches, one-half going to the sheriff as his voucher and the fitting or tallying half being kept as a check on his honesty. With his half-sticks and his bags of money appears the sheriff at the table. Challenges are heard; tallies are compared with their mates; coin is sampled, and perhaps taken by handfuls to the assay-room and melted on the spot; and then, with counters, coin, and tallies, the game is played from which the institution probably received the title Exchequer or "the checkers." The results of all these noisy comparisons of debit and credit are found, with the details of the accounts, in the old rolls known, from their appearance when laid away, as Pipe Rolls, a long and unbroken series of which is still in existence. If the account balanced, it was written off by the words *quietus est;* if not, the sheriff was accorded a brief and sorrowful extension, or immediately sent to prison.

MODERN ACCOUNTANCY

Modern Accountancy may be said to have become possible with the introduction and gradual adoption of rational methods of procedure in arithmetic and book-keeping. "It is horrifying," says a recent editor of an old set of accounts of an English abbey—"it is horrifying to modern notions to think of the trouble which was involved in arriving at these arithmetical results." The clumsy old Roman notation, which lingered along among the smaller tradesmen of England, Germany, and France until the end of the sixteenth century, necessitated the use of all sorts of expedients. In adding, one did not keep figures in his head as we do; he jotted down on a separate paper or parchment a number of C's and X's and V's, and counted the number of single strokes, and then "it was easy," we are told, "to tot up the amount." In Chaucer's day the counting-board was a matter of course—even when, as in *The Shipman's Tale*, he tells of the Accountancy of an enterprising French merchant. We find old Samuel Pepys learning the multiplication table of those days at least three years and a half after he becomes a clerk of the Exchequer. Even in Italy the so-called Arabic system, upon which mercantile arithmetic is founded, made way slowly, and not without opposition. As late as the beginning of the fourteenth century the bankers of Florence were forbidden by law to use the Arabic numerals; and the University of Padua, fifty years later, ordered that its books should be price-marked, "not with ciphers, but with letters"—*non per cifras sed per literas claras.* The Oriental system, however, gradually supplanted the Roman, so that it may be said that by the middle of the sixteenth century it was the arithmetic of the better class of merchants throughout Europe. Its operations, at first cumbersome, were afterwards improved by the simplification of the fundamental processes—by the introduction of plus, minus, and other signs, by the invention of logarithms, and by the use of the decimal notation for fractions.

Book-keeping, as distinguished from the mere memorandum form of entry belonging to the old notation, was described in the very first printed work on arithmetic and algebra, published at Venice in 1494 by Lucas Pacioli or Paciolus, otherwise known, from the Tuscan town of his nativity, as Lucas di Burgo. The older account-books, with their paragraphical arrangement, their headings and sub-headings, their sums and sum totals, were more picturesque and apparently more readable than the new scientific form with its tabular appearance. Besides, an easy change from the ancient notation to the new, with its decimal numeration, made it possible to carry all amounts out to marginal columns for convenience of calculation; this improvement appeared to many to be all that was needed. Thus arose the phenomenon, hardly worthy to be dignified as a compromise, entitled single-entry, to distinguish it from the debit-credit method of so-called double-entry. The new method, however, appealed to the practical mathematical mind, and, along with the mercantile arithmetic, won its way. It laid a foundation for the scientific study of the art of keeping accounts, and became in slightly varying forms the recording system of the nations —first, of Italy, then, under the influence of Simon Stevinus, in the national accounts of the Dutch and the French, last, as recently developed into Cerboni's logismography, in Italy again, its early home.

AUDITING

Auditing presents to our view, historically, a number of distinct phases. Roman law says that to audit is to examine accounts, but the examination may be interested or disinterested, perfunctory or hearty, and intelligent or otherwise; as the attitude, moral condition, and capacity of the examiner have an important bearing on the value of his report, the securing of a sound audit has been an economic problem. Auditors with almost judicial power are mentioned in an English statute of 1285; but the importance and diversity of later auditorship are results of modern business conditions. The present recognition of the scientific audit, in which is included the auditing of the auditor, is due to professional Accountancy.

ACCOUNTANCY AS A PROFESSION

Accountancy in the later professional sense includes not only a detailed and scientific knowledge of accounting and of books of account, and their relationship to one another, and to any form of business, but also the oversight and scrutiny of records and systems of record in the interest of honesty, order, facility, and clearness of comprehension. It includes, moreover, a comprehensive mental and mathematical grasp of a business enterprise in its totality and in all the inter-related details of its organization and conduct, for purposes of diagnosis, consultation, and suggestion. This is the result of a gradual evolution from business conditions and from the progressive intelligence of leading commercial nations, and cannot be credited to any one nation. Scotland has been said—by a Scottish writer in the *North American Review* for October, 1894—to have had a distinct profession of Accountancy, ranking with that of barrister, as early as the middle of the seventeenth century. This writer evidently referred to a class of men of the transitional period of calculating and recording, who kept and examined accounts, and not to Accountancy or to a learned profession as at present understood. The development of the profession, however, and its solid worth and respectability, are undoubtedly due in every notable measure to the accountants of Scotland; they were the first to secure royal charter, and their knowledge of Scottish commercial law, as well as of the art of accounting, is of a high order. The years of incorporation are: 1854 for the Society of Accountants in Edinburgh, 1855 for the Institute of Accountants and Actuaries in Glasgow, and 1867 for the Society of Accountants of Aberdeen.

England, however, has been looked upon as the home of modern public Accountancy. The numerical strength of the profession in southern Britain, its semi-conservative activity and, to some appreciable extent, the early commercial and financial necessities upon which that activity was fed, have stamped a special English trade-mark over the Scottish birth-mark of the chartered Accountancy of the empire. The real depth of gratitude owed by the whole empire of commerce to English Accountancy, properly so-called, is for the noble stand taken by the Institute of Chartered Accountants in England and Wales when, upon its incorporation by royal charter in 1880, it announced its objects to be "the elevation of the profession of public accountants as a whole, and the promotion of their efficiency and usefulness, by compelling the observance of strict rules of conduct as a condition of membership, and by setting up a high standard of professional and general education and knowledge." These words, from this source, brought

Accountancy within sight of its proper goal; they gave hope, as it spread to Ireland, the British colonies, the European continent, and the United States, to those who entertained worthy views of its exalted mission.

Professional Accountancy came to the United States with a rich inheritance of European tradition; it united itself with the eminently practical business science of the New World. Here it absorbed more and more of our best talent, saying and thinking less and less of English methods. With British and American advantages, however, it retained one peculiarly English imperfection— viz., the want of a place in the modern system of economic education. This English defect was to us all the more serious in view of our conservative reverence for the geographical source of our profession. But, while it may be said that England, with her Oxford and her Cambridge, has no worthy system of commercial education, we remember also that continental Europe, of whose higher commercial education we read so much, has made no special provision for scientific culture in professional Accountancy.

It remained, then, to American professional Accountancy to conceive and make a way, not only to the position indicated by the Institute in England in 1880, not merely to successive vantage-grounds in line with the progress of commercial science, but to its true educational and moral centre of life and activity at the fountain-head of the economic stream. It was seen that, following the crumbling away of the old apprenticeship system in the trades, there had been going on a readjustment of the conditions of clerkship in the professions; and that, as student life in the lawyer's and the physician's office was already united with study in the legal and the medical school, professional Accountancy, also, must have its co-ordinate system of college education along with its practical training in actual experience. At the request of the profession, New York, followed substantially by other States, enacted a law providing for a certificate of qualification to practice as a certified public accountant, with a penalty attaching to the fraudulent use of the professional designation C.P.A. Under this law was founded a State regency examination, presupposing a very fair knowledge of practical accounting, of the theory of accounts, of auditing, and of commercial law. At the further request of the profession, and in line with the present movement for economic culture, New York University now establishes, in its School of Commerce, Accounts, and Finance, the first university department in which the demand for professional education in higher Accountancy receives adequate recognition. And not the least of the services thus accorded to commerce and finance by the University is the blending of its facilities for academic instruction with the requirements of the world of affairs. With this foundation the profession of pedagogy is brought into the training of the accountant, without depriving him of his practical and professional associations; under the law the prospective accountant must have been connected for a time with an accountant's office.

THE LESSONS OF THE PAST

Our subsequent detailed investigation of eras and phenomena belonging to the past of Accountancy will furnish lessons invaluable in practical application; these will fully warrant the compacting of our historical material into a constructive science. The present panoramic view can hardly fail to suggest that there must be in the economic world a permanent place for professional Accountancy; that professional Accountancy is in worthy measure performing its mission; that it may look forward hopefully and courageously to a future of vast usefulness; and that the time is not far distant for the formulation of a code of professional ethics. This last consideration may not be so obvious to the present hasty historical glance as the others; but let it be remarked that the bare mention of professional aspirations, in the sense in which I have desired to be understood, involves a recognition of professional rights and responsibilties. Besides, wherever the light of history is clear enough to reveal the relationships of men and their doings, a line of right or wrong is seen to form one of the connecting threads. The relations of accountants to one another and to their clientele are analogous to those of the members of other learned professions; and the growth of Accountancy into a profession in the academic sense may be taken as an obvious historical argument for a similarly analogous code of ethics.

It will hardly need any argument aside from the most elementary view of history, though many proofs from other sources might be adduced, to show that in any respectable economic system there is a place for professional Accountancy. Everywhere, in proportion to the volume and activity of business, the expert accountant is a necessity. Even the great nations themselves in their corporate capacity, with their elaborate recording systems and their large forces of officials of financial control, are beginning to recognize independent expert Accountancy in the management of their accounts. The United States, a few years ago, to the immediate saving of six hundred thousand dollars a year, employed a couple of professional accountants to reorganize our entire governmental system of accounting; the London *Times*, only a few days ago, eloquently appealed to Great Britain to submit her national accounts to examination by professional experts. Municipalities, transportation companies, financial organizations of all kinds, great commercial houses, industrial corporations, all appreciate the economic value of professional Accountancy, and are on the scent, more and more keenly, for able investigators of their affairs. Books are to be looked into; fraud and error are to be detected and prevented; method and order are to be effected and preserved; adaptability, simplicity, lucidity, economy, are to be considered and achieved; and this is but the entrance, the outer vestibule, to the place that awaits the professional accountant capable of entering in. The entire enterprise is to be scanned, to be sounded, to be investigated; these services are to be rendered, not in any sense of ownership or administration of affairs, but in the light of profit and loss and general business health. A report is to be made—the report of a consulting physician who has felt the pulse, taken the temperature, and performed his auscultation, who knows its financial condition, its strength, its weakness, its bad habits, its expectation of life; this report must be courageous, must be morally, mentally, and actually true, and must be comprehensive, concise, and clear. Questions and cross-questionings, of owners, of stockholders, of directors, of presidents, are often to be answered as supplementary to the report; the answers must be intelligent, ready, and never resentful. These gentlemen desire truth and nothing else; it belongs to the spirit of professional Accountancy to seek out and reveal to them the truth. They desire, also, above all things, to comprehend fully any future course indicated as a result of the investigations; the accountant with capacity for comprehensive and thorough investigation is of incalculable value as an adviser. The place for Accountancy, having grown to these dimensions, is enlarging, and will continue to expand. We may say, in the light of the history of our profession, that its opportunities will be manifoldly greater and more numerous in the future than ever in the past.

Accountancy has so far kept fair pace with its opportunities, and is measurably meeting the expectations of the present. It has grown with the growth of modern business; it has sought to surround itself, in the interest of economic integrity, with moral and legal safeguards; it has made the same efforts looking to educational fitness, and under the same disadvantages as have the other economic sciences and modern professions; it has won, and continues to command, universal respect and admiration. Forecasting the future from the past, we may confidently prophesy the continued growth of professional Accountancy with the enlargement of its peculiar sphere of action; an expansion of moral and mental capacity in meeting its obligations, and an increase in favor with the world of affairs. Or, taking a more general sweep of view, we may say that a development which, so far as we know, has been steadily continuous from the beginning, will doubtless proceed indefinitely.

As we have seen Accountancy in the infant condition in which the Hindoo boy calculates with pebbles and a stick in the sand, or the Japanese lady thrums on a kind of numerical dulcimer, or the big boys of old England play checkers with the finances of a nation, unite itself with crude notation and then dissolve away into a rational arithmetic on which could be founded an intelligent art of book-keeping—as we have seen the rise therefrom of a practical science of accounts, and then of the various functions exercised in the practice of higher Accountancy—from this sweep of view we may gather hope of continued advancement and a bright prospect for the future of our profession. But the ideal conception of its true mission by the profession itself—a conception from within and not dependent upon extraneous exigencies—places Accountancy far outside the pale of all ordinary callings, and sets it upon a platform of its own as a learned profession, self-impelled to culture, to moral enlargement, and to scientific attainment; it lays a basis of confidence for every business enterprise that in professional Accountancy there is a self-centred soul of economic truth.

VIII

ACCOUNTANCY IN BABYLONIA AND ASSYRIA[1]

THE oldest existing records of financial and commercial accounting, so far as at present known, are found inscribed on the little hand-tablets of clay that are being dug up in south-western Asia. It is highly improbable that earlier business writings lie buried in the ruins of old Egypt or elsewhere; at present, at all events, we can safely assert that business archæology credits her most ancient treasures, not, as heretofore, to the valley of the Nile, but to the narrow strip of land lying between the Euphrates and the Tigris, where the grave of a lost and long-forgotten antiquity is yielding up a literature running back to the fourth millenium before this era. Accordingly, our history of Accountancy begins, at least tentatively, in what is commonly known as Mesopotamia, the country "between the rivers," styled with various latitudes of meaning, sometimes as Chaldæa, sometimes as Babylonia, sometimes as Assyria.[2]

[1] An unpublished essay.

[2] Chaldæa is properly the district in the extreme south, extending to the Persian Gulf; Babylonia is the district to the north of Chaldæa up to the point where the Euphrates and

We have already seen, in our introductory study of the history of Accountancy, that the quipu, the reckoning-frame, and the sanded abacus had, perhaps, a common Oriental origin; and this possible origin may have belonged in the Tigris-Euphrates valley. Occasionally, however, numerical errors appear in the documents under present consideration, which would seem to indicate the entire absence of all such arithmetical helps. On the other hand, these mistakes may have been due to clerical errors on the part of scribes, or even, though less probably, due to fraudulent falsification of accounts by collusion between interested parties and the learned official writers; and this falsification is rendered the more probable in view of the forward state of higher mathematics known to have been attained among the Babylonians and Assyrians. On the whole, we cannot say positively that we have or have not found here the more primitive Accountancy; and we are thrown back upon the mere statement that, so far as we know, the history of Accountancy begins among the so-called "bricks of Babylon."

THE NEED FOR ACCOUNTS IN ASSYRIA

The existence of a highly developed system of accounts among the ancient Mesopotamians would

Tigris approach each other for the first time; while Assyria is the northern portion along the banks of the Tigris.

naturally be suggested to us by our traditional knowledge of the glories of Babylonia and Assyria. Nineveh, the capital of the latter empire, appears to have embraced with its suburbs to the north and south a length of about eighteen miles along the bank of the Tigris, with an average breadth of twelve miles, and to have contained an area of more than two hundred square miles. We read in the Book of Jonah that Nineveh was "an exceeding great city of three days' journey." At the time this book was written, the city meant far more than the main portion opposite the modern Mosul. Babylon, the seat of the lower empire, in the days of the Neo-Babylonian empire under Nabopolassar and Nebuchadnezzar, acquired an extent and magnificence that rendered her the wonder of the world and of the ages. She is called in Isaiah (chap. xiii, 19), "the glory of kingdoms, the beauty of the Chaldees' pride." According to Herodotus, this powerful, splendid, and luxurious city stood foursquare on both sides of the Euphrates, sixty miles in circumference, protected by a high and massive wall, having a hundred prodigious gates of solid brass. These two cities, Nineveh and Babylon, were the queens of commerce of the ancient world. Various of the Hebrew prophets speak of the merchants of Babylon; Ezekiel (chap. xvii, 4) says that Chaldæa was a land of traffic, and Babylon was a city of merchants; and the prophet Nahum (chap.

iii, 16) tells us that Nineveh had multiplied her merchants above the stars of heaven. Had these and other buried cities of Mesopotamia, therefore, remained forever in their graves, had they never come forth at the call of modern archæology with their written records of an unparalleled commercial activity, we need not have hesitated to say, in the words of Professor Jastrow of the University of Pennsylvania, that "such commercial activity could not, as a matter of course, have been maintained without the perfection of a method of keeping a record of transactions."

RECORDS DISCOVERED

The resurrection of these records of a long-buried past, amounting almost to a miracle, is the astonishment of history. Berosus, a native priest, had written of the wonders of his country; Herodotus, the father of history, and other Greeks, had sung the praises of Babylonian greatness; the writers of the Bible, Josephus, and the Jewish sages of the Talmudical period had testified to her long-enduring grandeur; every school-child had read with eager imagination of the "pensile paradise" or hanging gardens of her wonderful seat of universal empire. But Babylon's glory was gone, and had left no trace; Mesopotamia, the land of great cities and of a wealth and commerce of unbounded extent, had been a wilderness for ages on ages. So utterly had Babylonia and Assyria been wiped off from the face of the earth that for long ages the world had not even known where to place the once proud cities of these powerful empires in the historical geography of the land, or how to arrange their kings or dynasties in its chronology. Xenophon, with his famous Ten Thousand, passed over the grave of Nineveh and didn't know it. Alexander the Great died in Babylon, yet his contemporary historians never mentioned the name of Nineveh. And, as in the upper country, so it was in the lower. Defeat, deportation, and plague had left Babylon a desolation, and decay had turned her into a desert in the midst of a desert. From one end of the land to the other every city had become an unknown heap of dirt, a grave without a gravestone. The story of the wonders of Mesopotamia had lost all its bearings of time and place, and it read like some fantastic tale of a country in the clouds. This weird unreality was heightened as we perused the eulogistic words of Herodotus, Ctesias, Diodorus Siculus, Quintus Curtius, Strabo, Pliny, and others in their descriptions of the walls, the palaces, the temples, the gardens, the canals, the quays, the tunnels, the bridges, the commerce, the treasures, the armies, and the dominion of these cities of a distant past. We saw as in a dream the flowing of the wealth of all nations into a kind of mystic Babylon; we beheld the coming thither of the caravans of merchants from Idumea, Syria, Sardis, Egypt, and Susa; we pictured the fortified stations and busy resting-places along the highways of the desert from Palestine and Arabia and on the great roads leading from Persia and Media; we saw the sailing of vessels up the Persian Gulf with their cargoes of gems, ivory, ebony, frankincense, spices, silks, and dyes, and the drifting of rafts down the rivers burdened with the goods of the mountain countries. And with the same half-slumbering consciousness we viewed the returning foreign traders laden with the sumptuous dress-goods and carpets of Mesopotamia.

The blank and awful desolation of this unfortunate land had long been the despair of the descriptive pen. The traveller, the historian, the trader, the geographer, the antiquarian, the tale-teller, the poet, and the preacher, all had endeavored in vain to realize to our imagination the irretrievable ruin of the old civilization of Mesopotamia. Pliny tells us that in his day Babylonia was "a perfect desert." Lucian, of Samosata, writing in the reign of Marcus Aurelius, mentions Babylon as a city once noted for its many towers and its great extent, "but which will soon," he says, "disappear as completely as Nineveh has disappeared." Jerome, some two centuries later, tells us he was credibly informed that Babylon had in his day become a royal hunting-ground for the killing of wild beasts of the desert. Mohammed, in the sixteenth sura of the Koran, doubtless alluding to a mound then supposed to represent the site of Babel, says that "God came into their building and overthrew it from the very foundation, so that the roof fell on them from above and a punishment came on them from whence they had not expected." Near this mound, in the Mohammedan town of Bagdad, was afterwards composed, or at least compiled, the story collection known as the *Arabian Nights' Entertainments*, a book dealing, when not occupied with the intrigues of women, in the knavery of slaves, the hypocrisy of dervishes, the corruption of judges, and altogether presenting a moral companion picture appropriate to the physical degradation of the land. The famous Jewish traveller Benjamin, of Tudela (1160); the geographer Ortelius, of Antwerp (1596); the Italian voyager Cesare de Federici, as translated for Hakluyt's collections (1599); Rauwolf, of Augsburg (1573); Babbi, a Venetian jeweller (1579); the English merchant Eldred; the explorer Cartwright, about the beginning of the seventeenth century; the Spanish ambassador Figueroa, of the time of Philip III.; the restless Portuguese merchant Pedro Teixeita; the eccentric Sir Anthony Shirley (1599); the Italian Pietro della Valle (1616–1625), who was the first to copy some cuneiform characters from monuments at Persepolis; Sir

Thomas Herbert (1626); the French traveller Tavernier (1644); Father Vincent, of Vienna (1657); Flower (1667); Chardin (1674); the German Engelbrecht Kampfer (about 1694); Cornelis de Brum (1701); Otter (1734); Edward Ives (1758); Emmanuel de Saint Albert (about 1700), in his Oriental report to the Duke of Orleans—all these and many other writers for hundreds of years have contributed to represent to us, between the Tigris and Euphrates, a broken, battered land, given over, town and country, to robbers, to prowling beasts and poisonous reptiles, to bats and owls and other doleful creatures. Rauwolf, more than three hundred years ago, in his Itinerarium[1] said of an old tower near the Euphrates: "It is so filled with venomous creatures that one can only approach it during the two months of their hibernation, when they cannot leave their lurking-places." Father Vincent, a century later, as he passed up the Euphrates, says: "We heard, to our terror, the roaring of lions answering one another from opposite banks of the river." Claudius Rich, excavating one of the mounds in 1811, says that in several parts of it "there are many dens of wild beasts." Layard says that in the country surrounding ancient Babylon "are found leopards, lynxes, wild cats, wolves, hyenas, jackals, deer, porcupines, boars in vast

[1] Published in Lanzingen, 1583.

numbers, and other animals." In his famous book on *Nineveh and Babylon* (N. Y., ed. 1853, pp. 486, 487), Layard says of the town of Hillah, now occupying a part of the site of Babylon, that lions were allowed to roam its streets unmolested. "One," he tells us, "was a daily customer to the stalls of the butchers, who, on his approach, made a hasty retreat, leaving him in undisputed possession. A large lion," he says again, "was in the habit of coming regularly every evening from the Euphrates to a canal which I crossed on my way to Babylon. He repeated his visits in search of prey till shot by one of the Arabs." It would seem, therefore, little short of a miracle that in this wild waste of surface, relieved by shapeless mounds of crumbling rubbish, depressed with erratic ruins of neglected canals, overrun by thieves and cut-throats, and hideous with all that is dismal of animal life, an authentic history should have been located and brought to light as the result of the modern scientific application of the shovel. That any mortal eye should ever again look upon the original record - books of her selling and buying of measures of wheat, of herds of cattle, of men and women in bondage, of houses and lands, of clothing, of jewels and trinkets, of manual labor, of brain - work, and of all merchandisable commodities and exchangeable interests— that these record - books should be found fallen from their shelves and scattered in confusion over the floors of her ruined counting-houses and archive offices was a thing beyond all dream or thought of human possibility. Never once had it entered the mind of the most visionary that sober, sedate history would sometime be called upon to record the unearthing of hundreds of thousands of the identical documents of record of all this mercantile activity.

The Euphrates and Tigris take their rise near together in the mountain regions of Armenia, and, flowing in a generally parallel southeasterly course over the highlands of ancient Assyria, through the Babylonian plain, and into the Chaldean swamplands, unite to form a short stream which empties into the Persian Gulf. Mesopotamia, the inter-river country, thus roughly named and defined, rocky and unproductive in the northwest, and naturally barren, but capable of the very highest condition of cultivation in its central and southwestern divisions, has been the scene, during the nineteenth century, of the most marvellous recovery of a lost history of which we have any knowledge. Of this recovered history the chapter on economics, including a fragmentary account of the oldest known methods of keeping track of debits and credits, is not the least important part; it will increase in importance and wonder as the "miscellaneous" or business documents of this high antiquity shall continue to yield up their secrets to the deciphering activity of modern linguistic experts. The full story of the unearthing and reading of the clay tablets of the Assyrio-Babylonians would be the biography of a hundred heroes of exploration and of scholarship, and is the province of many books to tell.[1] Searching, digging, and deciphering along the twin rivers of western Asia, from Nineveh to Babylon and on beyond Ur of the Chaldees, or poring over the little cuneiform records housed away in the great museums of Europe and America, such adventurous and learned Orientalists as Botta, Rich, Layard, Grotefend, Rawlinson, Hincks, Burnouf, Rassam, George Smith, De Longperier, De Saulcy, Oppert, Menant, Victor Place, Norris, Loftus, Taylor, Fresnel, Sayce, Halévy, Schrader, Delitsch, Hommel, Haupt, Bezold, Pinches, Strassmaier, De Sarzec, Brunnow, Jensen, Abel, Alfred and Friedrich Jeremias, Lehmann, Zimmern, Winckler, Tallqvist, Peiser, Meissner, Amiaud, Scheil, Budge, Evetts, Strong, King, Johns, Tiele, Lyon, Reisner, Muss-Arnolt, McCurdy, Harper, Price, Rogers, Craig, Jastrow, Thompson, Ward, Peters, Haynes, and Hilprecht, have patiently labored and are still toiling in order to lay before us from the royal, religious, and business libraries

[1] The most complete and satisfactory account of the early travellers, of later explorers, and of the gradual work of decipherment is to be found in Rogers's *History of Babylonia and Assyria* (New York, 1900), vol. i., pp. 1–253.

and literary storehouses of Khorsabad, Nineveh, Kalah, Sippar, Kutha, Babylon, Borsippa, Nippur, Erech, Telloh, Larsa, Ur, and other Mesopotamian cities, their many thousands of brick books on every subject known to the people of that hoary age.

The accounting records of Babylonia and Assyria form a part of the "miscellaneous documents" known by the unfortunate misnomer, "contract tablets." Of these miscellaneous records, including not only all kinds of social contracts of barter, sale, money-lending, hiring, renting, marriage dowry, wills, adoption of children, lawsuits, and the like, but also of memoranda, lists, inventories, entries of income and outgo in cash and in kind, written for the express purpose of keeping track of accounts and balances, we know as yet much less than we do of the more general literary, theological, political, and historical inscriptions. An increasing number of Assyriologists, however, are turning their attention to the study of these neglected records. Three or four important works devoted to certain collections of the miscellaneous tablets are now in course of publication,[1] and the more we are enabled to learn of the business documents unearthed in the Tigris-Euphrates basin the more clearly is revealed to us—to use the words

[1] Among recent works may be mentioned additional texts published by the authorities of the British Museum.

of Professor Lyon, of Harvard—"a state of affairs not essentially unlike that in which we now live."

CHARACTER OF RECORDS AND ENTRIES

It is an open question whether papyrus, palm-leaf, parchment, or some other writing - surface, handier than that of the clay tablet, may not also have been in familiar use. However this may be, the tablets of Babylonia were of clay, because clay, of the very finest quality, and readily hardening under the climatic conditions of the country, was the one free and inexhaustible material of the lower valley, where not a stone or pebble or stick of timber is ever found, and where the use of clay was universal, from the building of walls and palaces of cities down to the making of little balls used as weapons of warfare. In Nineveh and all the upper country, which was a land of rock, an utterly unnecessary use of clay prevailed, especially in laying the foundations of great structures, merely because the settlers from below had brought their traditional customs with them; among these customs the use of the clay tablet for writing remained; and it remained to the end, as it had remained from the beginning — whether Assyria ruled, or Babylonia was in the ascendency, or a foreign foe had taken possession of the land—because of the persistency of Chaldean civilization. This persistency is of material advantage in the very difficult investigation of the business methods of the ancient dwellers in this land, rendering available, as it does, the tablets as the representatives of one economic system lasting throughout all changes of dynasties. A written promise to pay, whether found by De Sarzec at Telloh (antedating by thousands of years the days of Abraham) or by Haynes at Nippur, or by other discoverers of instruments still two thousand years older, will be substantially the same in form as the British Museum tablets, written within twenty - five years of the birth of Christ, or as a note of hand in the Museum at Zurich, believed by Oppert to belong to the first century of our own era. For illustration, the following translation of this latest dated business tablet of Babylon is given, which it would take an Assyriologist to distinguish in form from a similar document of the days of Abraham: "Forty tetradrachma owed. Larassib, son of Bel-akhe-irib, will pay into the hands of Zir-Idin, son of Hablai, in the month Iyar, 40 tetradrachma, in the Temple of the Sun, in Babylon. Witnesses: Urrame, son of Ruya; Allit, son of Airad; Kistar, son of Sinam; Zir-Idin, son of Hablai, scribe. Babylon, month of Kislev, third day; fifth year of Pacorus, King of Persia."

A Babylonian library, or archive-room, or counting-house, may not unfitly be compared to a brick-yard. "It requires some effort," says Madame

Ragozin, the author of *The Story of Chaldea* (p. 109), " to bear in mind the nature and looks of the things which we must represent to ourselves when we talk of Assyrian books." "True," writes Professor Sayce,[1] "the books are written upon clay, and not on paper, but they are none the less real books, dealing with all the subjects of knowledge known at the time they were compiled." Layard, describing the brick books or tablets found by him at Nineveh, says: "They were of different sizes; the largest were flat, and measured nine inches by six and one-half; the smaller were slightly convex, and some were not more than an inch long, with but one or two lines of writing. The cuneiform characters on most of them were singularly sharp and well defined, but so minute in some instances as to be illegible without a magnifying-glass." "The contract tablets," writes Professor Budge, of the British Museum, referring to the miscellaneous tablets, among which are found the accounting records, "are of all shapes, oval, oblong, square; their color varies, sometimes black, then brown, dark and light, and all intermediate shades. Sometimes they are baked, often they are not." Speaking of the minuteness of the writing on many of the tablets, Professor Sayce infers that the scribes and readers of the Tigris-Euphrates country must have

---

[1] *Babylonian Literature*, p. 6

been decidedly short-sighted, and says that "we need not be surprised, therefore, to learn that Sir Austin Layard discovered a crystal lens, which had been turned on a lathe, upon the site of the great library at Nineveh." It ought to be said, however, that this lens is as often referred to an astronomical use as to that of a reading-glass. The instrument generally employed in tracing the characters on the fresh clay was a little rod with a blunt triangular end, which, being lightly pressed on the moist tablet, left a wedge-shaped, or cuneiform impression. These minute, wedge - formed impressions, variously slanted and combined, made up an elaborate and complicated alphabet, not of letters or sound-signs, but of syllables and word-signs. The tablet, if small, was held in the left hand during the writing; the rod or stylus in the right; and when one side was full, the tablet was turned over to be inscribed on the other. If it was large, it was found necessary to lay it upon a desk to be written on, and the surface already inscribed was protected by little pegs projecting from the clay as legs of a table, and these pegs served the same purpose during the baking of the tablet. The tablets that were not baked, including a very large proportion of the accounting documents, were readily dried and hardened in the sun. The more important tablets were impressed with a seal. Herodotus tells us that the seal of the Mesopotamian was as important as his name. It was buried with him when he died; Taylor found at Ur a skeleton having his seal attached to his wrist. The legal contracts were also signed with the names of several witnesses; those who could not sign made their mark with the impression of their thumb-nail. A large number of business tablets are found encased in a surrounding layer of clay, bearing a copy of the document inside. The records are generally arranged in some convenient order, being deposited together in such order in earthen jars, and, thus classified, they were laid away on shelves for reference and preservation.

EDUCATION OF THE ACCOUNTANT IN ASSYRIA

The question as to the spread of popular education among the ancient Assyrians and Babylonians has led to the expression of a number of somewhat surprising opinions. With an intricate and most difficult system of writing, the Mesopotamians, we are told by highly trustworthy Orientalists, were an educated people. "The contract tablets," writes Professor Sayce, the learned author of *Social Life Among the Assyrians and Babylonians*, "are written in a variety of running hands, some of which are as bad as the worst that passes through the modern post. Every legal document required the signatures of a number of witnesses, and most of these were able to write their own names." Again he says: "Women, as well as men, enjoyed the advantages of education; this is evident," he continues, "from the Babylonian contract-tablets, in which we find women, as well as men, appearing as plaintiffs or defendants in suits, as partners in commercial transactions, and, when need arose, signing their names." According to Sayce, also, "It is probable that boys and girls pursued their studies at the same schools," though it should be added that no definite evidence for the education of girls is as yet forthcoming. Expressing the opinion that the child's education began early, he adduces a very old non-Semitic nursery-tale to show that it did *not* begin before the age of five or six. In the highlands, we are told by the same writer, education was by no means so widely spread as on the plains; yet even here, he contends, "the upper and professional classes, including the men of business, as well as the public scribes, were possessed of the advantages of an advanced education." This subject of Babylonian education, however, is very comprehensive. The field is wide enough for many honest differences of opinion; and the more conservative scholars incline to the view that education in Babylonia and Assyria was not general; by such it is held that the acquirement of the art of reading and, certainly, of writing was confined to the priests and to the professional scribes who, likewise, belonged to the priesthood.   In a history of Accountancy the question is fairly confined to the bearings of this education on the accounting records found among the cuneiform inscriptions.

COMMERCIAL EDUCATION OF THE PEOPLE

Commercial education in Mesopotamia, speaking in the academic sense, certainly reverts to a high antiquity   From time immemorial, pedagogues existed "devoted to the training of novices in the art of reading and writing, in order to fit them for their future tasks as official scribes."   Maspero, the eminent French Orientalist, in his *Dawn of Civilization*, says of the education of the public scribe, that "he learned the routine of administrative and judicial affairs, the formularies of correspondence either with nobles or with ordinary people, the art of writing, of calculating quickly, and of making out bills correctly."   Professor Jastrow,[1] to whom I am indebted for friendly assistance in the investigation of this subject, says that while the Babylonian scribe was taught to aspire to the priesthood or to literary distinction, a large share of his education as a school-boy was in the direction of fitting him to be an expert in commercial affairs.   In the task of familiarizing himself with the many hun-

[1] See also his article "The Text-book Literature of the Babylonians" in the *Biblical World*, April, 1897, pp. 248–268.

dreds of combinations of wedge-letters he filled his little copy-tablet, not with child-language, but with words and phrases and sentences which would be of immediate practical use to him in keeping accounts, in drawing up formal agreements between seller and buyer, lessor and lessee, borrower and lender, in the preparation of contracts of marriage and of divorce, in writing out last wills and testaments, terms of adoption, of inheritance and disinherit-ance, legal decisions of judges, and the formal docu-ments in which disputing parties bound themselves to abide thereby, and in his choice of expressions connected with Mesopotamian business life. In the grammatical study of his mother-tongue, and in connecting its orthography with the still living word-signs of another and already extinct language, the student, instead of taking the sentimental verb "amo, amas," as we do in our classical studies, he was led at once, as it were, into the counting-house, and was taught to write with his little arrow-headed characters some such business word as "he weighed, they weighed, he weighs, they weigh"; and then to attach a suffix and make it read, "he weighed it, they weighed it, he weighs it, they weigh it." And so with "to measure, to divide, to pay," and other verbs, in all their forms and com-binations. Not "dominus, domini," and so forth, was given to the young scribe in the counting-house as his noun exercise, but some such word as "price";

and an old teaching-tablet still carries the modern student of Assyriology through such forms as "the price, his price, to his price, for his price he placed, full price, for his price in full, price not in full, for the future his price not in full"; and this tablet goes on to connect these phrases with several verbal forms, as, "he pays, he fixes" the price, and so on. Then the practical utility of these educational exercises is further increased by, let us say, a tablet treating the word for "hand," both singular and plural, in such a way that the student learns how to express all the variations of the idea of paying the price "into the hands, into their hands," and thus "into the treasury." Here is the way an exercise-tablet on the word for "income" prepares the young scribe to look after the interests of the temple of Shamash, the sun-god of the Babylonians—and let it be premised that this word for income means more literally an increase on capital: "Income, his income, to his income, to his income he placed, income of Shamash, income of Shamash is fixed, the income of Shamash he increased, the income of Shamash he places, the income of Shamash he gave, the income of Shamash he returns, without increase, there is increase, there is no income, the income is as that of the municipality, the increase has gone by default, the increase of the increase"—that is compound increase or interest—"there has been an increase of increase." Another tablet gives various forms of the verbs "to weigh" and "to measure," and then proceeds with "grain he has measured, he is measuring the grain, they are measuring the grain, he has not measured the grain, he weighs the silver, they are weighing the silver, he is not weighing the silver, the silver he weighs and the grain he measures." Thus, step by step, the young man is brought gradually, almost imperceptibly, forward in the use of his syllabary and his long list of logographs until, before he is aware of his own proficiency, he is actually duplicating the commercial literature of his native land, telling how much "silver he weighs out," that "the house for the silver he secures," that "when he had brought the silver he took possession of the house," and that "as long as he lives in the house he is to secure the beams of the house and to keep the walls in repair," all being phrases and sentences that occur in an extensive legal literature.

Along with this practical tendency of the study of the art of writing went that of the reckoning of numbers; and thus, many thousands of years ago, was realized in practice a pedagogical theory again suggested in our own day by Monsieur Lefevre, late private secretary to Baron Rothschild, who, in a pamphlet published some years ago, contended that "the first, or elementary, rules of accountancy belong to the domain of primary education; that they are more easily apprehended than those of arithmetic, to which they should lead up as question leads to answer or inquiry to discovery; and that with accountancy in this extreme simplicity as a foundation, the student easily advances to that which is more and more intricate, learning meanwhile habits of order, of classification, of method, and of analysis, discovering thereby his own improper tendencies, and preparing himself almost insensibly for the later study of whatever profession he may choose to embrace."

DEVELOPMENT OF MATHEMATICS

Accounting ability implies, of course, a knowledge of arithmetic; and "the Babylonians," says Professor Budge of the British Museum, "were essentially calculators." Their mathematics, however, is seen to better advantage in their astronomical achievements than in anything as yet discovered on the face of the business tablets. Lenormant tells us that, "next to grammar, the sciences most frequently met with on the tablets are mathematics and astronomy." Astronomy, indeed, had risen to the rank of a real science among the Chaldæans in the remotest ages, and its progress is generally admitted to have embraced all that was possible to observation with the naked eye, while--as we have seen it—it has even been suggested that Layard's lens discovered at Nineveh, is needed to

account for the wonderful advancement of Mesopotamian astronomy. This advancement embraced regular astronomical observations of planets
and fixed stars, of the phases of the moon, of the
risings of Jupiter, Venus, and Mars; calculations of
eclipses of the moon, and perhaps of the sun; the
division of the zodiac, the outlining of the constellation, the division of the day into hours, of
hours into minutes, and of minutes into seconds;
the foundation of their chronology upon a great
period of solar years, believed by the Babylonians
to represent the procession of the equinoxes; the
building of astronomical observatories, the issuing
of astronomical reports, and altogether a series of
discoveries and the possession of a fund of astronomical knowledge quite impossible except upon
the supposition of proficiency in mathematics.
True, this astronomy was always intermixed with
astrology; many hundreds of portent-tablets[1]—one
astrological work, compiled in the days of Sargon
I., whose date may be as high as 3800 B.C., containing not less than seventy tablets—give such
information as that "the moon being out of her
reckoning, the tariff will be small," that "the moon
and the sun balancing, the country is established,"

[1] See two important recent publications—*Craig's Astrological-
Astronomical Texts* (Leipzig, 1899), and Thompson's *Reports of
the Magicians and Astrologers of Nineveh and Babylon* (London, 1900, two vols.).

or, referring to the vernal equinox, that "day and night balancing, six double-hours of day to six double-hours of night, the gods are drawing near to my lord the king," and much more of the same sort. But astrology, especially the astrology which underlay the religion of the Chaldæans, implied, not less than the purer astronomy, an advanced knowledge of the science of mathematics.

We are prepared, then, to learn that many treatises on arithmetic have been discovered among the tablets unearthed in the various libraries. One tablet, dug out of the ruins of ancient Larsa, contains a list of the squares of fractional numbers correctly calculated from one-sixtieth up to unity. The Babylonians, in the indication of fractions, divided the unit into sixtieths, each of these again by sixty, and so on *ad infinitum.* "This," writes Lenormant in his *History of the Ancient Orient,* "was the result of a wise combination of the two systems of dividing unity that have been in dispute at all times and among all nations—the decimal and the duodecimal. Sixty," he continues, "is divisible by all the divisors of ten and of twelve, and is, of all the numbers which may be chosen as an invariable denominator for fractions, the one possessing the greatest number of divisors. Sexagesimal numeration," he still goes on, "regulated the scale of the divisions and of the multiples in the metrical system of Babylon and Nineveh, the wisest and best organized system in the ancient world, and the only system, previous to the introduction of that of France, in which all proportions were scientifically concordant with a fundamental plan of unities derived from one primitive and typical linear measurement." [1] This practical combination of the decimal and duodecimal systems characterized the Babylonian treatment of numbers throughout. Tables of cubes, as well as of squares, were also found at Larsa, which of themselves would show, as a recent writer remarks, that the Babylonians had need of very high numbers for some kind of reckoning; and a series of geometrical figures, used, indeed, for the purpose of predicting future events, nevertheless presupposes, as Professor Sayce has pointed out, "a sort of Babylonian Euclid." According to Lenormant (*History of the Ancient Orient*, Chevallier's translation, vol. i., p. 449), the division of the circle and of the chord, equal to the radius, into their several kinds of degrees, and the invention of a notation marking infinitesimal divisions of these degrees, are due to the Chaldæo-Assyrians. These are a few of the many indications of a forward state of mathematics among the

[1] The further complications of the numerical and astronomical system of the Babylonians and the bearings of astronomical news upon the religious symbolism and the mythology developed in the Euphrates Valley are concisely set forth in Arinckler's essay, "Babylonische Kultur" (Leipzig, 1902).

ancient people of the Tigris-Euphrates basin; and it is clear that both writing and arithmetic were at the service of the business man of Babylon, if not, indeed, at the tips of his fingers.

COMMERCIAL LAW

A third and most important branch of Babylonian business education was that of commercial law. The preponderance of legal documents among the business tablets is, indeed, so great as to have given to the whole body of this peculiar literature the indiscriminate title of "contracts." From the very earliest times of which we have any account the commercial life of the Babylonians is represented, in all its departments, by regulated forms and practices for the purpose of carrying out obligations and of settling mercantile and financial difficulties. The Babylonians, we are told, were emphatically a law-fearing people; and the precedents to which their judges appealed, as a recent English writer has remarked, would delight the heart of the student of Blackstone. An eminent French author has even ventured to suggest that a number of the disinterred tablets, representing contracts between private individuals, were intended to serve merely as *formulæ juris privati*. The bricks tell us much of the criminal laws of the sombre inhabitants of Babylonia and Assyria; but, as Lenormant has pointed out, they tell us more of their civil laws. The tablets have revealed to us not only a most remarkable development of law in general, but an elaboration of property laws in particular, which of themselves, had we failed of more direct information, would have demonstrated the existence of an immense and restless commerce and of some adequate system of Accountancy. And the monotonous regularity of form, age after age, given to the documents and vouchers filed away throughout the land, samples of which are now to be seen in the great museums of the Old World and the New, shows that nothing was done at hap-hazard, that every business transaction took place according to law, and that the commercial tablet-writer, public or private, was obliged to understand, and sometimes to apprehend very quickly and with fine discrimination, the established form for any required document connected with the transfer of property. Jastrow tells us that in the Babylonian system of commercial education special texts were in use for the better understanding of these formulæ and of the peculiar terms employed in preparing the legal and commercial tablets; and so tantalizingly technical are many of these terms that Professor Johns, in his recent work on *Assyrian Deeds and Documents*, says it may be long before they are completely understood, "or some genius shall arise who shall see through all difficulties at a glance." Jeremiah the prophet, writing of the recovery of Jewish real estate from the hands of the Chaldæans, correctly describes a tablet-deed, and the requirements of legal documents in general, when he says (chap. xxii.): "Men shall buy fields for money, and shall subscribe the deeds, and shall seal them, and shall call witnesses." So vast is the number, and so comprehensive the variety of existing records evidencing the legal erudition of the ancient Oriental writers of business tablets, that a mere sample or two must suffice for illustration. The disastrous attempt of the Assyrians upon Jerusalem, and the ignominious return of Sennacherib to Nineveh, are well known. Lord Byron says:

" The Assyrian came down like the wolf on the fold,
  And his cohorts were gleaming in purple and gold;
  And the sheen of their spears was like stars on the sea,
  When the blue wave rolls nightly on deep Galilee."

Herodotus says the Assyrians were defeated because, as certain Egyptian priests once told him, a host of field-mice came in the night and destroyed their bow-strings. The Biblical account is that the Angel of the Lord went through them in the night, and that "when they arose early in the morning, behold, they were all dead corpses." According to Sennacherib's own report, as translated by George Smith, the great king returns in dazzling triumph to Nineveh, while "not a single shadow

of reverse or disaster appears in the whole narra-
tive." He was murdered while at worship in his
temple; and among the inscriptions found at Nineveh was a document that is commonly known as
"the Will of Sennacherib":

"I, Sennacherib, King of multitudes, King of Assyria,
give golden chains, ivory in quantities, a golden cup,
crowns, and neck - chains; all these beautiful riches in
heaps; and crystal and a precious stone and a bird-stone
—one and one-half minas, two and one-half shekels by
weight—to Esarhaddon, my son, surnamed, acĉording to
my wish, Asshursarilikpan. The treasure is deposited in
the temple of Amuk. Thine is the kingdom, O Nebo, our
light!"

Royalty might dispense with the calling of witnesses; elsewhere, however, the most noticeable
feature of the legal tablet, to modern eyes, is the
remarkable number of attesting names appended
to the instrument. The following brief guarantee,
found at Nippur and translated by Professor Hilprecht,[1] is more than half full of proper names, including those of the tablet-writer and seven other
witnesses; and all to warrant a jeweller's stone
from falling out of a ring:

"Bel-ah-iddina and Belshunu, sons of Bel-muballit, and
Hatin, son of Bazuzu, spoke unto Bel-nadin-shumu, son
of Murashu, thus: 'As concerns the gold ring set with an

[1] *Business Documents of Murashu Sons* (Philadelphia, 1898),
p. 31.

emerald, we guarantee that for twenty years the emerald will not fall out of the gold ring. If the emerald should fall out of the gold ring before the end of twenty years, Bel-ah-iddina, Belshunu, and Hatin shall pay unto Bel-nadin-shumu an indemnity of ten mana of silver. Witness: Ninib-nadin, son of Ninib-erba; Nabu-mudammiq, son of Iddina-Marduk; Ardi-Ninib, son of Ninib-muballit; Dannia, son of Nadin; Iddina-Marduk, son of Uballitsu-Marduk; Ninib-ahe-bullit, son of Ahu-shu-nu; Ninib-ah-iddina, son of Bel-shum-ibni. The thumb-nail mark of Bel - ah - iddina, Belshunu, and Hatin, instead of their seal. Scribe : Ninib - na - sir, son of Ardi - Bel. Nippur, 8th day of Elul, 35th year of Artaxerxes,[1] King of Nations.' "

ARRANGEMENT OF ACCOUNTS

Thus we see that the Assyrio-Babylonians were possessed of a respectable working knowledge of writing, of reckoning, and of business law. We may reasonably expect to find also among their clumsy tablets, and, notwithstanding the possible loss of handier but more perishable records, an indication of their office administration of commerce, accounts, and finance. The astonishing antiquity of their commerce is seen in their economic study of an already extinct language, a vast pro-

[1] *I. e.*, Artaxerxes I. (464–424 B.C.) ; the document was, therefore, drawn up 429 B.C. Elul or Ululu is the sixth month of the Babylonian calendar, and since the year, consisting of twelve lunar months (with an occasionally interjected month) began in the spring, Elul corresponds, roughly, to August or September.

portion of whose words and ideas belong to the trade activities of a high civilization. In volume three, new series, of *Records of the Past* (pp. 91–101), Berton publishes translations of portions of a series of tablets, written in so-called Sumerian or Babylonian language, containing a compendium, not of laws, but of precepts and prescriptions drawn from the customs and usages of the most ancient times for the guidance of the people in their various professions; one chapter is on "precepts for a man in private life"; another has for its subject "agricultural precepts," and another treats on "commercial precepts."[1] The relics of Telloh and of Nippur are bringing before us an almost historical view of this commerce from the farthest Sumerian and Akkadian times to the days of the Semitic Babylonians, as it existed under their Assyrian overlords, under the Persians, under the Greeks, under the Parthians, under the Sassanians, and down, perhaps, to the early caliphs represented by the Cufic coins. It reached its fullest development in the eighth and seventh centuries before the Christian era. Sayce is of opinion that in geographical extent it stretched to India, whence the Babylonians had their ivory, or "wood of Sind,"

---

[1] Although it is doubtful, according to other scholars, whether what Berton takes for precepts are anything more than "copy" exercises for young students learning to read and write.

and to the Cornish coast, from which they brought their tin

VOUCHERS

From Father Strassmaier's publication of several thousand business tablets Dr. Zehnpfund of Germany [1] has recently extracted documents of the reign of Nabonidus, some fifty or sixty, all dealing with the one subject of clothing, and representing vouchers for raw material and for the manufactured articles of wearing apparel. These tablets, and the words found in the school-boy lists already mentioned, present a very large variety of garments and stuffs dealt in by the merchants of the old Tigris-Euphrates cities. Black garments, white garments, dark garments, green garments, and garments described as new, as old, as torn, as soiled, and the like, are specified, and many kinds of cloth are enumerated, some of them known from their place of manufacture or customary use—just as our muslin, or mousseline, is named from Mossoul, opposite ancient Nineveh. Then, according to Jastrow, we have in the text-book literature a number of words for different parts of the dress, for the cloak, for the tunic, for the head-gear, for the dress of the deity, of the king, of the queen, for the ceremonial prayer dress, for a fine dress, and one term

---

[1] *Beiträge zur Assyriologie*, vol. i., pp. 492–537.

that corresponds closely to our "evening dress." The variety and volume of this commerce, domestic and foreign, and its attendant industrial activity, was seen in town and country, and on river, land, and sea; and Diodorus Siculus tells us that along the banks of the Euphrates and Tigris were an immense number of warehouses for the storage of the manufactures of the country and its imported goods. Even in the more military North, the merchant was a leading figure, and the campaigns of the later kings were often directed by the interests of trade. Professor Rogers, in his recent *History of Babylonia and Assyria*,[1] tells us that in more than one instance the traders of the upper valley, who had invaded the whole East and were taking gain from buying and selling, and from transport and storage, influenced their king to conquest in order to increase the field of their operations and the extent of their money-getting. In the lower country, more devoted to the arts of peace, a man's worth was measured by his wealth, and the possession of money meant power and dignity. "Hence," writes Professor Sayce, "the keen interest taken in commerce by all classes of the community, from the king downward."

This extensive traffic would of necessity be accompanied by some more or less perfect system of

[1] Vol. i., p. 309.

accounting; accordingly, from the earliest to the latest ages into which the tablets carry us, we find the Mesopotamians engaged in making office records of their mercantile transactions. As might be expected, the common trade-tablets have often the appearance of being "hurriedly scrawled" and are usually sun-dried, though many of them, especially the more important, are well written on fine clay, and have been carefully baked. In the Metropolitan Museum of Art, in Central Park, New York City, may be seen an interesting example of this class of accounting records. It is a statement of liabilities, dated in the fourth year of Nabonidus, father of Belshazzar. The brick is light brown in color, about two inches wide by two and one-half in length, is badly cracked, and the clay has crumbled off in many places. But enough of the writing is still legible to show that the statement itemizes the debts of three men, whose names are given as Labashi, Lusananure, and Gimillu. This document is believed to have been issued by some agent, "through whose hands," says the modern editor, "the specified merchandise and money had to pass."

RECORDS EXPRESS TRANSACTIONS BY TALE

No certain traces have as yet been found of a coinage among this people before the time of the

Persian Darius.[1] Age after age, for thousands of years, the "money current with the merchant" consisted of pieces of silver, bits of gold, and of *lapis-lazuli*, thrown into the scales and weighed at each transaction. A brown hæmatite weight of considerable antiquity, discovered at Nippur, is marked "ten shekels of commercial gold." Grain was also a very important medium of exchange. The verb "to measure" meant, in general, to pay in kind by measurement, as "to weigh" meant to pay by weight in cash. A very extensive system of credit also prevailed, and Lenormant, in his classification of the instruments in use in Mesopotamia, some six hundred years before our era, mentions drafts upon one place payable at another, and cites among others the following, containing date of issue, date of maturity, and the names of all the parties necessary to a bill of exchange:

"Four minas, fifteen shekels of silver, of Ardu-Nana, son of Zakin, upon Mardukabalussar, son of Mardukabala-tirib, in the town of Orchoe. Mardukabalatirib will pay in the month of Tibil, four minas, fifteen shekels of silver, to Belabaliddin, son of Dennaidour, the 14th arakh-sam-ma, in the second year of Nabonidus king of Babylon."

[1] Jolins, in *Assyrian Deeds and Documents*, vol. iii., p. 8, is of the opinion that an expression "Ishtar heads," which occurs in connection with monetary transactions, may be the name of a rudimentary coin or ingots stamped with a head of Ishtar.

BANKING RECORDS

The documents of several firms, devoted entirely to monetary operations, have been recovered. Among these are the records of the house of Egibi & Sons, of Babylon, and the family of Murashu Sons, of Nippur. The working system of these magnates of finance and commerce embraced the transfer of balances from one account to another and the general use of a substituted currency performing the functions of money and convertible into the metal on demand or at a specified date. A carefully and methodically arranged office, said to be at least four thousand years old, has been discovered at Sippara, the Sepharvaim of the Bible. "This office," says the London report, "was a long chamber, round the walls of which was a row of slag shelves. Upon these shelves were arranged a number of wide-mouthed jars, each of which was closed with a tile fastened down with pitch. The tablets in each jar were found to relate to a definite series of transactions, so that each formed a primitive kind of deed - box or ledger. Some of the tablets were deeds of sale, leases, mortgages, and the like, and in some cases deeds had been deposited as security for loans, and it was necessary to attach codicils or memoranda to them. This was done by writing the memorandum upon a small clay tablet attached to a straw, and then sealing the other end of the straw to the larger tablet, a process not very different from that of modern times. The tablets relate to every class of trade and legal transactions, such as a large firm might carry on at the present time."

The office of Murashu Sons, discovered in 1893, is thus described by Professor Hilprecht, in the introduction to volume nine of the publications of the Babylonian expedition of the University of Pennsylvania:[1]

"While occupied in the exploration of the central part of the northwestern ridge of the ruins of Nippur, the Expedition came upon a room about 5.5 x 2.75m, about 6m feet below the surface.[2] Its ceiling had collapsed long ago, its side walls, for the greater part, were in ruins, and the clay floor was covered with earth and rubbish from above. A gang of trained Affej workmen was ordered to remove the débris that filled the room, when suddenly they noticed numerous clay tablets lying upon the floor. A few hours later the whole room had been carefully searched and cleaned. Seven hundred and thirty tablets were gathered and safely stored in the castle of our fortified camp. After a critical examination of the building itself, and of the condition, position, and contents of the tablets found therein, it became evident that the excavated room had been once used as a business archive by the apparently wealthy and influential firm of Murashu Sons, of

[1] Descriptive title—*Business Documents of Murashu Sons*, p. 13.
[2] About eighteen feet by nine feet, and about twenty feet below the surface.

Nippur, who lived in the time of Artaxerxes I. and Darius
II., in whose reigns the documents are dated. All these
tablets, covering a period of more than fifty years, and inscribed by many different hands in Nippur and neighbor-
ing places, were made of an especially pure and soft clay,
and moulded and baked with greater care than is usual
in the Babylonian tablets met with in my experience."

The Egibi tablets, which have been critically examined by Professor Pinches of the British Museum,
were the last acquisition made by the lamented
young wood-engraver and archæologist, George
Smith, who died of the plague while endeavoring
to reach England. They were found by some
Arabs, deposited in a number of earthen-ware
jars. They record the transactions of a banking
firm which carried on business from an unknown
period down to about 400 B.C. The name of
" Egibi" has been identified with " Jacob," though
this view is now regarded as improbable. But
it certainly represented a commercial house at
Babylon like that of Murashu Sons, indicating
thereby a tribal division of the lower Chaldæans.
The founder of the business firm is believed to
have lived as early as 1000 B.C. The existing
tablets cover a period of about one hundred and
sixty-five years. They are of various sizes, the
smaller being about three-fourths of an inch in
length by one-half inch in width, while some of the
larger bricks measure twelve by nine inches. They

are usually covered with writing on both sides, and sometimes on the edges. They are the checks, ticklers, securities, and an endless variety of writings of a moneyed institution having dealings with everybody, from the poorest freeman or the slave to the king of Babylon or of Persia. Professor Sayce, in one of his lectures, tells us that in the banking calendar of Egibi & Sons all the bank holidays, and even the "lucky days" and "unlucky days," are scrupulously recorded. A number of their tablets are the merest rough memoranda, while the larger documents record important transactions that have been set down with the greatest care and elaboration of detail. One of the former, a little private memorandum of a payment of tribute in the reign of Cyrus,[1] reads:

"Three half royal shekels; 95 royal shekels; tribute; month, Siranu; day, 24; year, 2, of Cyrus, King of Babylon, 'King of Nations.'"

Another, an elaborate document, goes on to tell with great particularity how that a certain father and daughter, of the race of Egibi, had bespoken a certain described double wheat-field, and five female slaves and their children, for another scion of the family of Egibi, and that on a said day this other scion, with a relation, brother of the above daughter, had taken possession of the property;

[1] *Records of the Past*, old series, vol. ix., p. 93.

but that this brother of the above daughter had spirited the slaves away into the hands of a spice merchant, wherefore now the said other scion demands of his aunt—probably the wife and mother of the above father and daughter — the said missing slaves and their children, or an equivalent. This interesting document, perhaps laid before the heads of the house as referees, was made out on the first day of the month of Airu, of the fourteenth year of the reign of Nabonidus, and was witnessed by representatives of the military, clergy, and others of the élite of Babylon.

One year previous to the recording of this Egibi claim, there was made in Babylon a little brick with which two thousand four hundred and fifty-eight years have dealt rather harshly, and which may now be seen, gray and broken, in our Metropolitan Museum of Art. It bears a mere entry of a debt of five shekels—less than four dollars—payable conjointly by two men into the hands of the daughter of a third man; but whether with interest, or what the debt was for, the condition of the tablet is said to forbid our knowing. In the same collection, and of date about a hundred and fifteen years earlier, is a very small yellowish tablet in a perfect state of preservation, which bears the entry of one mina six and one-third shekels loaned, without mention of interest or date of payment, by one Shalu to one Belahirba, in the city of Himeri, on the twenty-fifth of Shabatu, in the twelfth year of Shamash-shum-ukin—about 657 B.C.

Hand-in-hand with commerce went agriculture, a principal source of Mesopotamian wealth and an important factor in Babylonian Accountancy. The inhabitants of the alluvial plain were distinctively an agricultural people, and their land, under an ideal system of cultivation, became proverbially productive.

Their vast labyrinth of canals, with its watergates and breakwaters, as Lenormant has pointed out, assisted in the defence of the country, afforded a means of complete inter-river communication, and "spread fertility in every direction." Irrigation, in the hands of this industrious people, was carried to a high pitch of perfection; their methods of agriculture, "transmitted," says Maspero, "first to the Greeks, and afterwards to the Arabs, were perpetuated long after their civilization had disappeared, and were even practised by the people of Irak under the Abbasside Caliphs." When Herodotus had looked upon the sea of grain that filled this land with plenty—blades of wheat and barley "four fingers in breadth"—he fully believed the report that from two hundred to three hundred measures were harvested to the measure sown. The yield was enormous, and measured grain, as we have seen, along with the balanced metals, was a recognized medium of exchange. Aside from this fact, and in the more modern sense, the wheat market was a feature of the trade activities of Babylonia, while dealings in future embraced all the principal crops of the soil. The Accountancy incident to these transactions may be illustrated by a description of two tablets, secured by Dr. Ward, of the Catherine Wolfe expedition, and which have been examined by the brothers Moldenke of New York.

RECORDS AND TRANSCRIPTS OF PRIVATE TRANSACTIONS

One of these is a little brown brick, a couple of inches long and about an inch wide, and which seems to be an accounting memorandum of the business house of a man of the name of Dinna, debiting one man to twelve measures of dates, which dates ought to have been delivered at harvest-time, and debiting another man, described as a son of King Nabonidus, to a whole crop of dates "not yet received," and crediting other debtors by two hundred and four measures of dates "received."

The other document, an elaborate account of a transaction in grain, dated the ninth day of the month Abu, in the ninth year of Nabopolassar, King of Babylon, is recorded, says Dr. Moldenke, on a hard, surface-glazed, gray tablet less than two inches wide by three inches in length. The gardeners of the temple of the sun-god Shamash

208

have sold this grain to the prefect of the province, and three men are selected to attend to its transportation by water. Below this statement a horizontal line is drawn across the clay. Then we are told that "in the first business transaction" the prefect pays no freight because the two ships used are his own; then another line is drawn. Next, the prefect uses another ship of his own and pays no freight. After another line drawn across the tablet, seven ships and their owners are specified. In the footing up of the ten cargoes an error of nearly sixty measures of grain occurs, to the detriment of the temple. Under another horizontal line the disbursements of the prefect are recorded, the scribe, for his intellectual work, receiving three times as much as the measurer, and the freight, or what we would call toll—for no money enters into the account—being altogether about one-third less than what the prefect has pocketed by the error in footing up the cargoes. Between this account and the final date on the tablet are written two other entirely separate accounts, and as nothing could have been written after the drying of the clay, two, and perhaps all three, of these accounts may have been copied from previous memorandum bricks.

Chaldæan pastoral life, along with agriculture, carries us back to the hazy confines of an utterly impenetrable antiquity. Already, in the days of clay tablets, written long before the shepherd Abraham of Ur had led his flocks up along the Euphrates and down the Jordan and around to the Nile, the raising of stock in the Mesopotamian valley had assumed immense proportions, and the keeping track of this species of property had brought with it its own Accountancy. The Hoffman collection, in the General Theological Seminary in New York, consists of two hundred and sixty-two bricks and fragments found at Telloh, Erech, Nippur, and Babylon, and covering a period of three thousand years, beginning about 3500 B.C.[1] A number of them are accounts of live-stock, showing how many head compose the flock or herd of certain specified keepers, and how many have been removed by expenditure, by sacrifice, and by death, with various charges to profit and loss. Very often the customary formulæ appear, while the figures are left out or erased, thus showing that the maker of the tablet got into the habit of writing ahead, while the stock was being counted, intending to insert the numbers before the clay should harden. Then follows the total of the stock received, the total removals, the name of the shepherd, and sometimes that of his overseer, the name of the city where the tablet is written, and the date. One of these accounts, of date about 2650 B.C., reads as follows:[2]

[1] Described in part by Radau, *Early Babylonian History* (New York, 1900), pp. 321–434.
[2] Radau, *loc. cit.*, p. 359.

"One hundred and sixty-nine ewes, 181 grown sheep, 43 she-lambs, 60 he-lambs, 2 weaned kids, present; 10 ewes, 8 grown sheep, 1 lamb, by Ab, head overseer, and 2 he-lambs, by Ur-Gula, head overseer, taken away; and 73 ewes, 11 grown sheep, 3 lambs, snatched away.[1] Total, 455 received. Total, 21 taken away. Total, 87 snatched away. Galumene. Tikabba city. Year that King Bursin devastates Urbillum."

PUBLIC ACCOUNTS

The support of religion and of the government gave rise to an enormous volume of business, which, in the case of the priesthood at least, was altogether commercial and which called for a vast accounting force. The education of the scribe, as we have seen, was eminently practical in the character of information imparted and sacerdotal in its ultimate aim. Jastrow has said, in a recent magazine article, that the Babylonian scribe was, in almost all cases, also a priest attached to one of the numerous temples that were found in all cities. The offerings of the people to the gods, reaching, according to Sayce, to the dignity of tithes, would have overflowed the storehouses had not a means been devised of utilizing them; the priests, therefore, says Maspero, "treated them as articles of commerce, and made a profit out of them." This business, it must be remembered, was carried on by

[1] "Charged off."

a body of men, each of whom was at once a theologian, a financier, and a trained accounting officer.

The royal administration again, according to Maspero's *Dawn of Civilization*, called for fiscal storehouses in town and country, and for a body of functionaries known as administrators of grain, administrators of the precious metals, of the fowl, of the herds of oxen, and so on—as many kinds of chiefs or administrators "as there were cultures or industries in the country." Among the more ancient expense lists now in the Hoffman collection, and cited by Radau[1] in a recent work on the early history of Babylonia, is a tablet of the time of Dungi III., King of Ur, who reigned about 2700 B.C., stating on one side how many shekels of money flowed into the treasury to the credit of different persons, and going on, after carrying forward the total to the other side, balancing the account by charging up for the amounts of grain bought with the money thus received.

FORMS OF BOOK-KEEPING

We have now seen that this people of the land of the two rivers, Assyrians or Babylonians or Chaldæans, had possessed from unknown ages an Accountancy which they were able to apply with

---

[1] *Loc. cit.*, p. 324.

a fair degree of success to the control of their domestic and foreign commerce, of their banking and
general financiering, of their agriculture and past-
urage, of their tithes and taxes, and of all the
material interests attaching to their political, religious, and economic life and institutions. And we
have seen in a general way the form it assumed
under the limitations of the clay. Looking more
particularly to the physical form of this Accountancy, we shall be impressed with its likeness to
much that has appeared under better circumstances. Dr. Moldenke, translator of a number of
the bricks in the Ward collection in New York,
compares the appearance of one of them to that
of a modern ledger, and says that its author "evidently kept a careful account for each day." This
tablet is of a mauve color, about two by three and
one-half inches in breadth and length, and records,
on one side only, the cattle and sheep presented to
each of the gods in the sun-temple at Sippara on
the thirteenth day of the month Airu, in the thirteenth year of King Nabopolassar. Beneath this
general statement of the object and date of the tablet a horizontal line is drawn, and the rest of the surface is divided into three columns by two perpendic-
ular lines drawn near the left edge. Headings are then
placed at the top of the narrow left-hand columns,
and, lastly, with cuneiform figures and with blanks
for "ditto," the fourteen divinities are properly

charged with their sacrifices for that day. In the
Columbia University collection of clay tablets are
a number of very ancient ruled inscriptions from
Telloh, some of which, believed to be general accounts of receipts and expenses of the temple, remind us forcibly of the primitive single entry of our
own Middle Ages. In Arnold's monograph on these
temple records,[1] attention is called to an error in
the first total of the following account; otherwise
it will be seen that the additions are correct:

> 85 sheep at $1\frac{1}{2}$ measures.
> 104 sheep at 1 measure.
> An expense of 235 measures.
> 88 sheep at $1\frac{1}{2}$ measures.
> 98 sheep at 1 measure.
> An expense of 230 measures.
> 42 lambs at $\frac{1}{2}$ measure.
> An expense of 21 measures.
> 10 head of cattle at 8 measures.
> 15 head of cattle at 6 measures.
> An expense of 170 measures.
> Balance in hand, 5 measures.
> Month of Shu-Kue.[2]
> The total for 30 days."

TECHNICAL LANGUAGE USED

To this Accountancy belonged a number of
technical terms or words used in an accommodated

[1] *Ancient Babylonian Temple Records* (New York, 1898), p. 5.
[2] Corresponds to the later Duzu, or fourth month.

technical sense, analogous to those of our own accounting system, and forming, as with us, a part of the business language of the people. Dr. Radau, in a recent description of the tablets in the Hoffman collection,[1] has given the original of many of the early words of this terminology, as, for example, how many sheep are "present," how many are "absent" or have been "taken," what wool, at the *lal*, or "selling," has been bought "of" or "from" this or that shepherd "for" so much money and "for," or for account of, such or such a weavery, and so on. And when we consider that from one end of the land to the other woollen as well as linen fabrics were important articles of manufacture, that the woven stuffs even of the farthest north, dyed in the most brilliant colors, were celebrated throughout the whole ancient world; when we consider again that the "weavers" were but one of the many classes of industrial organizations of this commercial people, we shall have some faint appreciation of the importance of that accumulation of business words with which our best Assyriologists are as yet confessedly least familiar.

CONCLUSION

The completion of this system would seem, in the present state of our knowledge of the subject,

---

[1] See p. 212.

to have required an extensive use of the legal documents in connection with the plainer tablets of accounts. Of the employment of papyrus or parchment in Assyrio-Babylonian Accountancy we are almost hopelessly ignorant; the constant use of the clay, however, would indicate the absence of a better writing material or the presence of a traditional superstition which prevented its adoption. Of the tablets of accounts, however, we cannot as yet contend that they give us an adequate view of the working system of this wonderful people; and until a much larger amount of this peculiar literature shall have become popularly accessible, it may be well to assume a twofold use of the legal records—one as contracts and the other as documents of accounts—to be used along with the account lists proper. In this view we shall have an Accountancy including three or four interesting safety methods. This is not so great a stretch of the imagination when we reflect that whatever was to be written on the brick must be written speedily and at once, before the surface of the quick-drying clay should harden. It follows, therefore, that an accounting brick, containing one or two entries, would often be not more of an account tablet than would many a legal contract, and that the duplication of the latter for accounting purposes would have been unnecessary.

The clay of this business literature, clumsy and

unwieldy as it was, had this advantage, that a word or figure inscribed and dried thereon could never be changed. A correction might be made at the time—and bungling attempts at correction made thousands of years ago in the soft clay are said to constitute one of the present difficulties of decipherment—but the account once written, and the clay once dry, no falsification could ever take place. Another element of safety was the clay envelope, or what is known as the "case tablet."[1] The more important documents, after baking, were surrounded with a coating of soft clay, which was inscribed with a duplicate of the inner record and then baked in its turn; and in case of controversy this outer envelope, as a last resort, was clipped off and the inner record was read in open court.[2] After being duly certified to by seals, or nail-marks, these records of this old economic history were classified and filed away on shelves and in earthenware "safes," to be audited thousands of years afterwards by the modern scientists of Assyriology.

[1] See John's *Assyrian Deeds and Documents*, vol. iii., p. 3.

[2] It should be noted, however, that the two copies rarely represent complete duplicates in matters of detail. The spelling generally varies in the two texts, and clauses are at times found in one copy which are omitted in the other. As a rule, the outer text is the more complete. See John's, *loc. cit.*, p. 4.

IX

THE MUNICIPAL ACCOUNTS OF CHICAGO[1]

MUNICIPAL history has not been able, as yet, to trace the origin of Municipal Accounting. Accounting records, on the other hand, are a principal source of municipal history. When we have exhausted our chronology of civic life, we are still in a civic world of indefinite antiquity but of very definite accounting methods covering adequate systems of financial administration. Ur of the Chaldees and her daughter cities, buried in their own débris and silent as to their beginnings and as to the establishment of primitive urban organization, are sending out from their desert tombs innumerable records of municipal debit and credit, inscribed on burned clay and dated in such and such years of unknown kings, which in form are startlingly modern. Away off eastward of Mesopotamia the Chinese know more about their old counting-frame than they do of their traditional first horde of wanderers in the forests of Shan-se—"houseless, naked, cold, eating raw meats and roots and insects."

[1] A paper read at the Seventh Annual Meeting of the National Municipal League, Rochester, New York, May 10, 1901.

And across the wide waste of the Pacific the knotted strings of the Peruvians recorded municipal revenue much more reliably than municipal history. Westward of Babylon a brighter star would seem to have taken its way. Xenophon tells us that Crœsus, in surrendering his immense riches, gave Cyrus an exact account in writing of the whole, containing the particulars with which each wagon was loaded, and that they were delivered thus at the palace in Babylon. Even the poor, perishable papyrus can tell us more of Egyptian accounting than the pyramids can of Egyptian origin. Wax tablets are coming down from the ages to assist us in reconstructing the financial routine of classic municipal administration. And the split sticks and other paraphernalia of the old English Exchequer take us back to the very forks of the road in our research into our own ancestral financial history, beyond which we know not whether to turn to the Briton, the Saxon, or the Norman.

REASONS FOR THE TARDINESS OF ACCOUNTING RE-FORMS IN THE UNITED STATES

With all this, remembering that many of the oldest existing records are the accounting records of ancestral cities of long-gone civilizations, it may seem incredible that we know so little of early American Accountancy. The perishability of paper, and the little interest taken until recently in municipal study, will partly account for our present want of historical knowledge of American municipal accounting; while the extreme simplicity of pioneer life, and the great fire of 1871, will further explain the absence of early municipal records of Chicago. The corporation records were at first kept, for want of books, on loose pieces of paper. The city's account-books that had accumulated to October, 1871, were destroyed in the great fire by which the municipality lost two and a half millions of dollars. Many county account-books of interest to the city have disappeared in other ways, special assessment collection cash-books, for instance, having been quadrennially destroyed. Neither county nor city treasurer has any ante-fire records. The city Comptroller's accounting records were all destroyed in the fire, and the new set was based on the printed report for 1871.

While the Constitution of the United States was being drawn up in convention at Philadelphia, the ordinance establishing the Northwest Territory was passed by Congress in the City of New York. This territory was afterwards divided into Ohio and Indiana. From the territory of Indiana were formed Indiana, Michigan, and Illinois. The territory of Michigan was again divided into Michigan and Wisconsin. Wisconsin would have included Chicago, but that upon the admission of Illinois

into the Union the boundary-line was shoved north
to give the new State a few miles of lake frontage.
And thus the chief lake port of the world is included in Illinois. Chicago to-day is about equal in
numerical size to all Wisconsin, or to all Illinois
outside of the city.

Illinois became a State in 1818. The present
constitution was adopted in 1870. Certain pro-
visions of this constitution have very seriously
affected the accounts of the City of Chicago. The
provision relating to the limitation of 'municipal
indebtedness is indefinitely worded, and has been a
source of serious complication and litigation. Laws
have been founded upon it by the State Legislature,
and have been declared unconstitutional by the
Supreme Court. According to a recent decision,
the debt limit is 5 per cent., not of the full valuation
of taxable property as ascertained by the assessment, but of the assessed valuation itself; or 1 per
cent. of the full value of assessed property. Chicago
has already exceeded the limit as thus defined; and
so one of the richest cities of the world, prohibited
by State authority from issuing bonds for necessary
improvements, remains, as has been stated by Mr.
Giles, of the Civic Federation, at a former conference
of the National Municipal League, in a deplorable
condition—with dirty streets, in need of light, having no garbage or street-cleaning plants, with public
buildings in shocking need of repair, and with life,

property, and health insufficiently protected. A most unhappy result to Chicago of this lingering paternalism is an unwilling parsimony of local financial administration treading dangerously close upon the heels of the integrity of municipal accounting. But accounting or no accounting, it would seem that there are some things a municipality must have, and to have must buy, and to buy must pay for. Treasurer M'Crae, of Edinburgh, used to tell of a new member of the council under the old system who moved to strike out an estimate of fifteen thousand pounds for wood for paving a street. "You may move as you like," said the convener of the committee, "but the wood has been bought and paid for." And so, account as you like, but Chicago knows how to anticipate revenue; or, if there is no money in the special wood fund, to generalize it out of any special coal fund that may be handy. Anticipatory scrip was issued in the year of town organization; it was common in the panic year when the town became a city; it is issued to-day in the form of temporary tax warrants and water certificates; and its market price has long been a kind of barometer of Chicago's credit.

ANTIQUATED METHODS OF CHICAGO

Cook County was organized in 1831, and Chicago became the county seat. The revenues were derived from licenses and a direct tax levied by the court. One-half of 1 per cent. was levied "on town lots, on pleasure carriages, on distilleries, on all horses, all mules, and all neat cattle above the age of three years, on watches and their appurtenances, and on all clocks." This was the simple method of seventy years ago. At present, according to a recent statement by the Citizens' Association, Cook County has three hundred and seventeen separate tax-imposing bodies, consisting of county, school districts, villages within towns, town governments, park boards, and the sanitary or drainage district. Many of these, some partly, some wholly, are within the city, while several of them, according to Professor Gray, of Northwestern University, go beyond the boundaries of the county itself. Their relationships to one another present a composite picture of independent, semi-dependent, and dependent financial administration anything but reassuring to the student of municipal accounting. It is said that this anomalous administration might legally hypothecate 25 per cent. of the assessed valuation of property in Cook County. These Cook County conditions amply justify the statement made by Mr. Hurd at the Milwaukee conference of the National Municipal League. "Some two years ago," he said, "I was talking with the President of the Board of Cook County Commissioners on the question of reform accounting. He gave it to me as his opinion that such a system once inaugurated would save the taxpayers of Cook County at least a million dollars a year; and I have no doubt that that opinion is within the limit."

Chicago, before the organization of Cook County, was successively in the counties of St. Clair, Madison, Clark, Pike, Fulton, and Peoria. The local tax collector in 1823 defaulted in the sum of $11.42; and this—the total levy—being one-half of 1 per cent. of $2284, we thus know the full valuation of all real and personal property, except household goods, at that time in the little settlement. Under a general act of 1831, the first meeting of the board of town trustees was held in 1833. The first city charter was granted in 1837, a second charter in 1851, a third in 1863, and the fourth and present city charter, so-called, that is, the general Cities and Villages Act of 1872, was adopted in 1875. The total population in 1812, swept away by the Indian massacre, had lived in five houses; at the time of town incorporation the population was less than one hundred and fifty; the Cities and Villages Act has seen Chicago's population increase sixfold to its present two millions—not counting, of course, an immense floating population. Dr. Shaw has selected Chicago, Liverpool, and Glasgow as excellent instances of the self-made, self-located modern commercial city, as contrasted with great urban communities like New York and London, which latter have assumed, he says, "vast proportions and importance in spite of themselves and without the application of any organic municipal energy."

According to an unpublished book, kindly loaned me by Dr. Maltbie, the original town area was three-eighths of a square mile. Numerous extensions have brought the city's area to one hundred and eighty-seven square miles, with an extreme width of fourteen and one-half miles and an extreme length of twenty-six miles. Pre-existing organizations, however, have been left intact, and other corporations, with municipal powers, have been added; thus, within this territorial extent of Chicago is now found an aggravation of Cook County chaos such as no man has yet been able to describe.

CONFLICTS OF JURISDICTION AND ACCOUNTABILITY

Nobody, for example, agrees with anybody else as to how many taxing bodies there are in Chicago. Professor Gray says nineteen—peculating, wasting, quarrelling, fighting, and constantly appealing to the legislature and to the courts. Mr. Giles says three distinct governments, with a dozen different taxing powers, which, for the purpose of raising insufficient revenues, unequally distribute burdens of taxation in many cases greater than the property can bear. The lawyers of the Civic Federation sum up twenty municipal or quasi-municipal corporations, some partially dependent upon the city machinery, others entirely independent and acknowledging no authority to control their actions except the constitution and the general assembly. The recent report to the Merchants' Club says that "there are at least twenty - one different taxing bodies in the city—the city council, which levies taxes for city, school, and library purposes; the drainage board, five separate park boards, the State, the county, the North, South, and West towns, and the towns of Lake View, Hyde Park, Lake, Jefferson, Evanston, Maine, Norwood, Niles, and Calumet." And this list might have been extended, the Board of Education and the Library Board, for example, being practically independent as taxing institutions. Some of the multifarious taxing bodies in Chicago are of no earthly use except to be buried. Many of them overlap one another, while in other places territory is omitted, thus forming an imperfect geographical system. The result of this, overtaxation on the one hand and exemption on the other, is a most unequal burden. A few of them extend beyond the city limits. One, indeed, goes beyond in one direction and comes short in the other. None of the independent taxing bodies is conterminous with the metropolis. On the whole, the resulting "shifting incidence of taxation" is worthy of another essay from the pen of Dr. Seligman.

It has been said that one may take his stand on

any street corner in Chicago and find himself amenable to at least five different governments, and that "each one takes him and filches him, but gives him little in return." The Comptroller, in his annual report recently issued, says: "If the different taxing bodies—that is, the park boards, the county, the town, the schools, the library, and the drainage boards, were consolidated into one government in the present limits of the City of Chicago, not only would there be centralized responsibility in the administration of public affairs, but there would also be great saving in the cost of this public administration." The Mayor of Chicago, in his last annual message, insisting upon a civic effort to make Chicago "a cheap city to live in and to do business in," and commending the present insistent agitation for municipal consolidation, urges the "welding of the present taxing bodies exercising municipal functions within the limits of Chicago into an harmonious whole, by which useless officers may be dispensed with, and all the various municipal functions be combined intelligently under individual control." Dr. Sparling well expresses the opinion of the local officials, taxpayers, business men, and students of municipal finance, when he says that "the conditions prevailing in the City of Chicago must find their ultimate solution in a consolidated and simplified charter, which will subordinate all the varied administrative interests, scattered among towns, parks, and municipality, under one central responsible organ." It will be readily understood that the administrative confusion resulting from the presence of this collection of heterogeneous intramural bodies, and from the city's crude relations to the county and the State, has a vital, not to say fatal, connection with Chicago's accounts and methods of accounting. No one knows better than the officials of Chicago's Department of Finance the truth of Mr. Ford's remark in the current *North American*, that it is "no easy task to shake the grasp of the country districts from the throats of the cities."

THE MOVEMENT TOWARDS REFORM

The question of reform in municipal accounting became prominent in Great Britain about seventy years ago. The *Quarterly* for January, 1834, urged the necessity of "requiring the parish accounts to be kept in a methodical and accurate form, such as will convey clear and correct information to those who audit them, as well as to Parliament and statisticians investigating the subject, on the real character of the several payments. At present," the writer continues, "all is confusion and perplexity. Each parish—nay, every successive overseer—has his own method of entering and keeping his accounts, intelligible to no one but himself." The movement throughout America, so far as it has yet made headway, is due in very large measure to the efforts of the National Municipal League; and "Chicago," said Mr. Sikes, at the Columbus Conference, "should get as much benefit from the League as any other city in the country." For, as Dr. Wilcox has written, "Chicago furnishes perhaps the best example of any American city where localism"—and he might have added paternalism —"has brought confusion and inefficiency."

The application of cold accounting to the burning question of municipal reform in Chicago is due to the business sagacity of the Merchants' Club—a young and sturdy organization of public-spirited citizens, working in harmony with the efforts of many of the city officials, including the Mayor and the Comptroller. Some months ago the Merchants' Club requested of the Mayor permission to have an investigation of the city's accounting methods made by a firm of experts. The investigation occupied about six months. The report was presented by the club to the members of the city council. An order in council was thereupon passed, calling for a mixed commission to devise a plan for a department of audits and accounts. The order has been vetoed by the Mayor on the ground that the Haskins & Sells Report calls for immediate action by the existing finance committee, and not by any dilatory mixed commission; this, the Mayor says, would only "discover the same old mare's nest, while but little real benefit to the city would be accomplished." Our last information is that the question of reformed accounting in Chicago was before a standing committee of the council itself for immediate action.

A DETAILED STATEMENT OF CONDITIONS, WITH REFORMS PROPOSED

Municipal accounting, as distinguished from general business accounting, is non-capitalistic—that is, the city's financial affairs do not involve, as their chief feature, the outlay of capital with a view to profit. All governmental accounts, however, ought to be controlled, organized, and handled with a view to efficiency of financial administration. They should enable any intelligent party in interest to follow the flow of money from the time it leaves the pockets of the taxpayers to the time it enters the pockets of those for whose services and supplies it is paid out. This control, organization, handling, and showing of accounts will be more or less dependent upon the organization and administration of the city government itself; it should also take account of traditional customs and habits involving, sometimes, a kind of subserviency to parties not properly in authority.

Chicago has a unicameral council consisting of the Mayor and seventy aldermen, who, with the clerk, attorney, and treasurer, are elected, while all other officials are appointed. But the Mayor's appointive power, seeming to promise a definite placing of administrative responsibility, is restricted, and his accountability vitiated, by an opposing power of aldermanic approval and disapproval. Nearly all the city officials are salaried; a few receive a percentage compensation. A salary, as compared with the free service of the League's ideal alderman, may not be the fittest compensation. But certainly the survival of the very unfittest is in the fee system now in operation in the office of Chicago's treasurer, who, with his official force, may be said to be almost another semi-independent taxing body. The Comptroller, appointed by the Mayor with the permission of the seventy, is theoretically at the head of the fiscal affairs of the city; and the Department of Finance might reasonably have been held responsible for the existing condition of the accounts, had not an accumulation of various complexities rendered it impossible for any set of men to bear upon their shoulders the blame that would accrue from the present state of the books. All moral charges may be laid to what by courtesy we must call the system or the methods; credit should be written up in full to the individuals, official and lay, who are laboring to bring about a betterment of Chicago's financial administration.

The taxes of the city proper, except delinquent

taxes, are payable to twelve town collectors; these are supposed to turn them over to the city treasurer upon demand made according to the existing revenue law. The city collections made by the town collectors appear in lump in the annual report of the county collector. The town collectors, however, delay these remittances to the utmost—thus profiting by the use of the money—and the city, while waiting, borrows money at a high rate of interest. For this equivocal service these town collectors are allowed a percentage up to a certain maximum; but for some years they have retained the percentage on the entire collection, the excess for the last five years over and above $90,000 allowed them by law being nearly $300,000. This irregularity forms one of the strong arguments for the utter abolition of the whole township system within the limits of Chicago.

Delinquent taxes and tardy special assessment collections go to the county collector, who is also county treasurer, and whose duty it is to remit to the city treasurer every ten days. The county collector, as in the case of the town collectors, also retains the use of the cash in his hands much longer than the period allowed by law, while the city borrows at such interest as it may. He has customarily reported tax deficiencies and losses to the extent of about half a million dollars a year; and these, for the past decade, have been charitably written off without question or verification. This custom is one of the arguments for a reorganization of the county and for the establishment of a board of audit in the city.

Revenue from licenses, water rates, special assessments, and miscellaneous sources, including income from franchises, is collected by various city officials and is deposited with the treasurer; these are reported to the Comptroller, except the miscellaneous revenue, which the Comptroller himself collects. Some of these receipts are very tardily reported, and some are not itemized. The franchise books are in a chaotic condition; their accounts are not audited, and a few of the large debtors make no payments for five or more years at a stretch. The condition of the special assessment accounts has rendered necessary the suspension of all payment on rebates, amounting to some millions of dollars, until a complete reconstruction of the whole from the date of the great fire shall have been effected. "Too severe a criticism," said the Comptroller in his Report for 1897, "cannot be made upon the lack of system prevalent, and the absolute neglect to post the books and accounts in the special assessment bureau of the department of public works. It was discovered that the books and accounts of that bureau were more than five years unposted, and your Comptroller was forced to refuse to honor any vouchers for the payment of rebates because of his inability properly to check the correctness of such vouchers from the books of that bureau." The reconstruction of these special assessment accounts is now in progress in the City Hall under contract with the city executive. The work will occupy some forty men about ten months, at a total cost of $65,000. It necessitates a patient and extensive research into original documents and records and a radical readjustment and complete rewriting of the accounts. A perfect record is to be made of every warrant, and the accounts are to be so arranged as to make them convenient for public use, "so that whenever inquiry is made by a citizen entitled to the information, the record of warrants and all other records relating to the special assessment accounts will be accessible and convenient for ready reference." This reconstruction will enable the Comptroller to resume payment in the matter of the special assessments and to make full settlement from the time of the fire of 1871.

The city's expenditures are incompletely recorded; debits are often wanting in detail; even the manner of payment is in some cases almost absurd. The incompleteness is largely due to lack of full departmental reports to the Comptroller; the want of detail is traditional, and the methods of payment are conveniences of the treasurer's office, which is run as a quasi-private counting-house. The police,

for instance, are called off post to receive their little envelopes at such places as the treasurer may
choose to station his pay-wagon. The constant
insubordination and assertion of independence on
the part of the treasurer have led to a movement to
extend the abolition of the odious fee system to his
office and to put his services on a salary basis.
Under the present fee system he is bonded in a
sum of fictitious importance, which, however, really
renders him subservient to a clique of private
bondsmen. The suggestion is that as a properly
amenable salaried officer he be bonded in a reason-
able amount, underwritten by a security company
whose interest it would be to extend to him all the
benefits of a personal audit, expecting to pay the
bond honestly in case of default. Chicago's accounts, considered in their entirety, are wanting in
uniformity. One department has one method, another department has another method; sometimes
an experimental method will be adopted, soon to
be superseded by another as evanescent. An outline of a well-rounded plan of accounting, in harmony with the system suggested by the National
Municipal League, has been laid before the Merchants' Club, and will doubtless be adopted, sooner
or later, by the municipal authorities. Responsible
control of accounts, also, as well as uniformity and
unity, is indispensable to the safe handling of public
funds; it has been further urged, therefore, as al-

ready intimated, that the council make immediate provision for the establishment of an adequate system of surveillance under a bureau of audit. The absence of a settled system of audit of Chicago's accounts is directly responsible for the interminable, tedious "battle of the books," in which many an honest reputation has been wounded, if not killed outright. Officials have wrestled with the crude accounts as best they might, and each has come to his own conclusion; one has reported one amount, and another has reported another amount, until nobody knows whether debts are increasing or decreasing, or what the real expenditures have been, or what the assets are worth. Only a few days ago three sets of books were found to contain the same account, in which each differed from the other two, and not one of them was correct.

THE POSSIBILITIES OF THE NEW SYSTEM

The recent investigation of Chicago's accounts has shown that about half a million dollars a year can be saved to the municipal treasury by the immediate adoption of certain reforms comprehended within the legitimate sphere of higher Accountancy. These reforms would include a proper investment of the sinking funds now in the hands of the treasurer, the doing away with the fee system prevailing in the treasurer's office, the enforcement of the present laws relating to the cost of gathering the taxes, the prompt collection and distribution of special assessment warrants, the auditing of statements made by tax-gatherers, the better accounting for taxes stayed and for tax purchases, and a general change in the method of collecting taxes and special assessments.

Beyond these reforms, an enforcement of the ordinances relating to franchise collections is urged. These suggestions are over and above the recommendation to establish an up-to-date system of accounts and audit, the value of which is beyond all estimate. The money value of the elimination of the town organizations would be at least a quarter of a million of dollars a year. The examination has further shown the wisdom of the present agitation for a new charter and for such constitutional amendment as will put the city in the way of looking after its own finances in its own way. The Honorable Lyman J. Gage has said that at least 80 per cent. of the people of his adopted city of Chicago desire honesty in administrative conscience; this fact would seem to completely overthrow the only respectable argument for State interference in the city's financial administration. Besides, as the same eminent authority has reminded us, "there is no reason to suppose that if the people had not virtue and capacity enough to get good government for themselves they can get any help from the people of the rest of the State, who are not so very much more virtuous or wise, and who have immeasurably less at stake." It is, therefore, devoutly to be wished that the popular agitation for legislative enactment and constitutional amendment looking to Chicago's financial prosperity may be crowned with the success due to the stubborn exhibition of municipal patriotism on the part of its citizens.

Chicago's motto is, "I will!" Civic pride is organized in numerous clubs, associations, leagues, and federations of business and professional men, laboring harmoniously for the betterment of municipal conditions. Nobody in Chicago is ever discouraged; the more dolefully one talks, the more earnest enthusiasm is brought out by reference to cities which have been reformed by means of the active co-operation of citizens. These gentlemen read with gusto such words as those of Mr. Martin, of London, in the current issue of the *Forum:* "Americans," he says, "who work for a nobler city government regard the London County Council as a pattern of ability, integrity, and enterprise that can only be vainly longed for on this side of the Atlantic; but, for their encouragement, they should recall the fact that not many years ago the government of London was the worst in Great Britain— unrepresentative, backward, dishonest, a subject of scorn and scoffing, and a by-word among provincial rulers." And Mr. Martin should be regarded as high authority, for he was an official of a borough in which another "council of seventy" has taken the place of about one hundred and fifty extinct bodies. Glasgow, also, has the respect of Chicago reformers; but we have been reminded, quite recently, by a delegate from the good Quaker town of Richmond, that people leave Glasgow and go to Chicago—they do not go from Chicago to Glasgow. And this assertion of Mr. Foulke's was corroborated in the person of a reverend Glasgow-Chicago gentleman who heard the statement. Chicago has agitated so many reforms, and has so often succeeded, that a member of the real-estate board of that city, speaking at a former conference, said, "If you will come to Chicago you will find in operation every system that has been outlined here as good." This, as Mr. Farr was reminded, was somewhat of an overstatement. Much, however, has been accomplished, and still the agitation for reform goes on. Having now taken up the question of Municipal Accounting, and struck therein the key-note of present Municipal Reform, it may be confidently expected that the citizens of this great interior metropolis will persistently hammer away at the problem until there shall be a practical recognition of the vital connection between finance and accounts, accounts and audits, audits and reports, and reports and public confidence.

THE END

THE DEVELOPMENT OF
CONTEMPORARY ACCOUNTING THOUGHT

An Arno Press Collection

Baldwin, H[arry] G[len]. **Accounting for Value As Well as Original Cost** *and* Castenholz, William B. **A Solution to the Appreciation Problem.** 2 Vols. in 1. 1927/1931

Baxter, William. **Collected Papers on Accounting.** 1978

Brief, Richard P., Ed. **Selections from Encyclopaedia of Accounting, 1903.** 1978

Broaker, Frank and Richard M. Chapman. **The American Accountants' Manual.** 1897

Canning, John B. **The Economics of Accountancy.** 1929

Chatfield, Michael, Ed. **The English View of Accountant's Duties and Responsibilities.** 1978

Cole, William Morse. **The Fundamentals of Accounting.** 1921

Congress of Accountants. **Official Record of the Proceedings of the Congress of Accountants.** 1904

Cronhelm, F[rederick] W[illiam]. **Double Entry by Single.** 1818

Davidson, Sidney. **The Plant Accounting Regulations of the Federal Power Commission.** 1952

De Paula, F[rederic] R[udolf] M[ackley]. **Developments in Accounting.** 1948

Epstein, Marc Jay. **The Effect of Scientific Management on the Development of the Standard Cost System** (Doctoral Dissertation, University of Oregon, 1973). 1978

Esquerré, Paul-Joseph. **The Applied Theory of Accounts.** 1914

Fitzgerald, A[dolf] A[lexander]. **Current Accounting Trends.** 1952

Garner, S. Paul and Marilynn Hughes, Eds. **Readings on Accounting Development.** 1978

Haskins, Charles Waldo. **Business Education and Accountancy.** 1904

Hein, Leonard William. **The British Companies Acts and the Practice of Accountancy 1844-1962** (Doctoral Dissertation, University of California, Los Angeles, 1962). 1978

Hendriksen, Eldon S. **Capital Expenditures in the Steel Industry, 1900 to 1953** (Doctoral Dissertation, University of California, Berkeley, 1956). 1978

Holmes, William, Linda H. Kistler and Louis S. Corsini. **Three Centuries of Accounting in Massachusetts.** 1978

Horngren, Charles T. **Implications for Accountants of the Uses of Financial Statements by Security Analysts** (Doctoral Dissertation, University of Chicago, 1955). 1978

Horrigan, James O., Ed. **Financial Ratio Analysis—An Historical Perspective.** 1978

Jones, [Edward Thomas]. **Jones's English System of Book-keeping.** 1796

Lamden, Charles William. **The Securities and Exchange Commission** (Doctoral Dissertation, University of California, Berkeley, 1949). 1978

Langer, Russell Davis. **Accounting As A Variable in Mergers** (Doctoral Dissertation, University of California, Berkeley, 1976). 1978

Lewis, J. Slater. **The Commercial Organisation of Factories.** 1896

Littleton, A[nnanias] C[harles] and B[asil] S. Yamey, Eds. **Studies in the History of Accounting.** 1956

Mair, John. **Book-keeping Moderniz'd.** 1793

Mann, Helen Scott. **Charles Ezra Sprague.** 1931

Marsh, C[hristopher] C[olumbus]. **The Theory and Practice of Bank Book-keeping.** 1856

Mitchell, William. **A New and Complete System of Book-keeping by an Improved Method of Double Entry.** 1796

Montgomery, Robert H. **Fifty Years of Accountancy.** 1939

Moonitz, Maurice. **The Entity Theory of Consolidated Statements.** 1951

Moonitz, Maurice, Ed. **Three Contributions to the Development of Accounting Thought.** 1978

Murray, David. **Chapters in the History of Bookkeeping, Accountancy & Commercial Arithmetic.** 1930

Nicholson, J[erome] Lee. **Cost Accounting.** 1913

Paton, William Andrew and Russell Alger Stevenson. **Principles of Accounting.** 1918

Pixley, Francis W[illiam]. **The Profession of a Chartered Accountant and Other Lectures.** 1897

Preinreich, Gabriel A. D. **The Nature of Dividends.** 1935

Previts, Gary John, Ed. **Early 20th Century Developments in American Accounting Thought.** 1978

Ronen, Joshua and George H. Sorter. **Relevant Financial Statements.** 1978

Shenkir, William G., Ed. **Carman G. Blough: His Professional Career and Accounting Thought.** 1978

Simpson, Kemper. **Economics for the Accountant.** 1921

Sneed, Florence R. **Parallelism in Two Disciplines.** (M.A. Thesis, University of Texas, Arlington, 1974). 1978

Sorter, George H. **The Boundaries of the Accounting Universe** (Doctoral Dissertation, University of Chicago, 1963). 1978

Storey, Reed K[arl]. **Matching Revenues with Costs** (Doctoral Dissertation, University of California, Berkeley, 1958). 1978

Sweeney, Henry W[hitcomb]. **Stabilized Accounting.** 1936

Van de Linde, Gérard. **Reminiscences.** 1917

Vatter, William J[oseph]. **The Fund Theory of Accounting and Its Implications for Financial Reports.** 1947

Walker, R. G. **Consolidated Statements.** 1978

Webster, Norman E., Comp. **The American Association of Public Accountants.** 1954

Wells, M. C., Ed. **American Engineers' Contributions to Cost Accounting.** 1978

Worthington, Beresford. **Professional Accountants.** 1895

Yamey, Basil S. **Essays on the History of Accounting.** 1978

Yamey, Basil S., Ed. **The Historical Development of Accounting.** 1978

Yang, J[u] M[ei]. **Goodwill and Other Intangibles.** 1927

Zeff, Stephen Addam. **A Critical Examination of the Orientation Postulate in Accounting, with Particular Attention to its Historical Development** (Doctoral Dissertation, University of Michigan, 1961). 1978

Zeff, Stephen A., Ed. **Selected Dickinson Lectures in Accounting.** 1978